semantics,
linguistics,
and
criticism

CONSULTING EDITOR: Richard Ohmann, *Wesleyan University*

semantics, linguistics, and criticism

WILLIAM H. YOUNGREN

Boston College

RANDOM HOUSE   NEW YORK

410
y79s

ISBN: 0–394–31309–7

Library of Congress Catalog Card Number: 72–144005

Typography by J. M. Wall

Manufactured in the United States of America. Composed by
Cherry Hill Composition, Pennsauken, N.J. Printed and
bound by Halliday Lithograph, West Hanover, Mass.

First Edition

9 8 7 6 5 4 3 2 1

Cover design by Fred Troller   73- 7118

ACKNOWLEDGMENTS

Excerpts from Alfred Korzybski: *Science and Sanity: An Introduction to Non-aristotelian Systems and General Semantics*, 1st ed. 1933, 4th ed. 1958 International Non-aristotelian Library Publishing Company, Dist. by Institute of General Semantics, Lakeville, Conn. Reprinted by permission of the Alfred Korzybski Estate.

Excerpts from *Language in Thought and Action*, 2nd Edition by S. I. Hayakawa (New York: Harcourt Brace Jovanovich), copyright 1941, 1949, © 1963, 1964, by Harcourt Brace Jovanovich, Inc. Reprinted by permission of Harcourt Brace Jovanovich, Inc., and George Allen & Unwin Ltd.

Excerpts from S. I. Hayakawa, "The Self-Image and Intercultural Understanding, or How to Be Sane Though Negro," copyright, 1953, by S. I. Hayakawa. Reprinted from his volume, *Symbol, Status & Personality*, by permission of Harcourt Brace Jovanovich, Inc.

Excerpts from Stuart Chase, *The Tyranny of Words*, copyright © 1938, 1966, by Stuart Chase. Reprinted by permission of Harcourt Brace Jovanovich, Inc.

Reprinted from Max Black, *Language and Philosophy: Studies in Method*. Copyright 1949 by Cornell University. Used by permission of Cornell University Press.

Excerpts from LANGUAGE by Leonard Bloomfield. Copyright 1933, by Holt, Rinehart and Winston, Inc. Copyright renewed © 1961, by Leonard Bloomfield. Reprinted by permission of Holt, Rinehart and Winston, Inc.

Excerpts from Ferdinand de Sassure, *Course in General Semantics*, reprinted by permission of the Philosophical Library.

Excerpts from Jerry A. Fodor, "Review of the Diversity of Meaning," *The Journal of Philosophy*, Vol. LXI, No. 11 (May 21, 1964). Reprinted by permission of the author and publisher.

Excerpts from Jerrold J. Katz, "Mentalism in Linguistics," *Language*, Vol. XL (1964). Reprinted by permission of the author and publisher.

Excerpts from Jerrold J. Katz and Jerry A. Fodor, "The Structure of a Semantic Theory," *Language*, Vol. XXXIX (1963). Reprinted by permission of the authors and publisher.

Excerpts from Jerrold J. Katz, *The Underlying Reality of Language and Its Philosophical Import*, xeroxed monograph.

Reprinted from *An Integrated Theory of Linguistic Descriptions* by Jerrold J. Katz and Paul Postal by permission of the M I T Press, Cambridge, Massachusetts. Copyright (c) 1964 by the Massachusetts Institute of Technology.

You think that after all you must be weaving a piece of cloth: because you are sitting at a loom—even if it is empty— and going through the motions of weaving.

WITTGENSTEIN

This book had its beginnings about eight years ago, when my friend Thomas Wilcox, of the University of Connecticut, asked me to edit an anthology of readings on language for a series of which he was general editor. At that time I was teaching English at M.I.T. and had become interested in what was happening there in linguistics; and since for some years I had also been very interested in contemporary linguistic philosophy, I saw the anthology as a splendid opportunity to bring together, for other people in literature with similar interests, the writings in these two other fields that I had found most provocative.

When I thought about an introduction to the anthology, it occurred to me that general semantics would be a good point of departure. For while the direct influence of Korzybski and his followers was not nearly as strong as it once had been, I was convinced that it was still to their books that most teachers of English usually turned for answers to the large theoretical questions about language that lie outside the proper subject matter of linguistics—questions about how language works and how it is related to the outside world. Moreover, I had an ulterior motive. Many years before, at Amherst College, I had taken a baffling freshman English course which, it was rumored, was based on general semantics, and the experience had left me with a curiosity about Korzybski that I had never fully satisfied. But once I began exploring the philosophical assumptions and implications of general semantics, I was led on to read more and more not only in philosophy, but in linguistics as well. The more I read, the more I wrote, and the anthology was gradually abandoned in favor of a book which would start with an examination of general semantics and then go on to elucidate what I took to be the most important relations of linguistics and linguistic philosophy to literary criticism.

I should here like to thank the many friends whose criticisms of one or another part helped me gradually to see how I wanted the whole to develop. Of these I am especially grateful to Bernard Haggin, to whom I owe an intellectual debt so pervasive and long-standing that it is almost impossible to specify; to Professor Wilcox, without whose unfailing patience, kindness, and tact I could never have finished; and to Professor Richard Ohmann of Wesleyan University, who not only offered useful criticism of my manuscript but also helped to get it published. I am also grateful to Professors Noam Chomsky and Jerrold Katz of M.I.T. for allowing me to attend their classes, and to the M.I.T. Department of Humanities, which for eight pleasant years gave me the opportunity to do just the sort of teaching and thinking that I needed to do, and which on two occasions, with the aid of the Old Dominion Foundation, granted me a semester's leave. Finally, I am grateful to my wife Virginia for many kinds of much-needed support, but most of all for her painstaking reading of the whole manuscript and her many suggestions as to how I could clarify the argument and clean up the prose.

William H. Youngren

NORTHAMPTON, MASSACHUSETTS
MARCH 1971

PREFACE

CONTENTS

In exactly the same sense that we may say the thought of the seventeenth century was dominated by mathematics and that of the nineteenth by biology, we may say the thought of the twentieth century has been dominated, so far at least, by language. Not only have individual human languages been investigated and analyzed by professional linguists with a thoroughness and precision unimaginable in the last century; language and linguistic considerations have also come to seem central to such diverse fields as psychology, sociology, anthropology, theology, law, political theory, genetics, education, and philosophy—and even to some forms of engineering!

We have, for example, heard a great deal about the crucial use of propagandistic language by totalitarian regimes. And to many suspicious laymen (and some professionals) the whole course of philosophy over the last thirty years or so has seemed a process of withdrawal from a serious concern with the most important age-old human questions to a frivolous fussing about mere words. The two most disastrous wars in human history and the development of a psychology concerned mainly with the unconscious have combined to undermine the traditional definition of man as the rational animal and to induce many linguistically oriented thinkers to redefine him as the language- or symbol-using animal. And as we shall see later, mechanistic determinism, the great nightmare of the late nineteenth and early twentieth centuries, may even be said to have been replaced by linguistic determinism. Instead of being trapped in a physical world indifferent and perhaps even hostile to his values and aspirations, a world that science has allegedly shown to be "a dull affair, soundless, scentless, colourless; merely the hurrying of material, endlessly, meaninglessly,"[1] man is now often seen as trapped (perhaps

[1] Alfred North Whitehead, *Science and the Modern World*

even more humiliatingly) within the categories imposed upon experience by the grammar of the particular language he happens to speak.

Why this great and pervasive shift of attention to language came about, I do not pretend to know; one can trace it in particular fields, but the general reason remains a mystery. That it has come about is, however, indisputable; and that it has raised at least as many questions as it has answered is scarcely less open to dispute. The creation of so-called ideal languages by logicians has made us nervous about the adequacy (or lack of it) of our own ordinary, unideal languages. The revelation that all natural human languages, including those once supposed to be most primitive, are of the same order of complexity and are thus absolutely different in kind from the most sophisticated communication systems employed by other animals has thrown the vague old evolutionary theories about the origin, and ultimately the nature, of language into a cocked hat. The complementary revelation of just how various languages are has made us sharply and disconcertingly aware of what was comfortable commonsense knowledge for every seventeenth-century writer on the subject: that verbal symbols, unlike most other sorts of signs or symbols, are completely arbitrary. The more we have come to know about language, the more baffled we have become.

One important result of this bafflement has been an increasingly strong desire for syntheses that will make clear the precise relations among the various ways of considering language systematically, a desire attested by the number of books that attempt such syntheses and by the number of conferences and symposia at which people occupied with language from different points of view are brought together to talk to one another. This is of course one of those

---

(New York: Macmillan, 1925), p. 77.

books, but I must add immediately that the synthesis it attempts is a rather limited one. The twentieth-century's concentration on language has raised special problems for the reader of literature, the man Dr. Johnson was fond of calling "the common reader": it is with those problems and that reader that I am concerned here.

Ever since Aristotle's *Poetics* many people have felt that the ordinary kind of description, interpretation, and judgment of literature that we now call criticism was in itself somehow inadequate, that it stood in need of some sort of theoretical buttressing if it was to attain the full status of knowledge. In fact the history of philosophical aesthetics is largely the history of the attempt to supply such buttressing, not only to the criticism of literature but to that of the other arts as well. Since about 1800 this sense of criticism's inadequacy has deepened into widespread conviction. For reasons that are all too clear from the words of Whitehead I quoted a moment ago, all but the very hardiest writers seriously concerned with literature, and particularly with poetry, have in one way or another felt challenged by science in the last century and a half. If the world really is that sort of world, of what possible use can it be to read or talk about poetry, particularly poetry of the remote past? How can such talk possibly be seen as anything more than the mere expression of arbitrary whim? Many literary men have responded to this challenge by saying that if science couldn't be licked, it should be joined—and have then gone ahead and attempted to do just that. But such compromise efforts have always ended in disappointment. One reason is surely that, like the efforts of I. A. Richards in the twenties to turn criticism into a species of psychology, they have always too obviously involved making one thing into something else that it obviously was not, and common sense has finally rebelled.

But now the growing domination of thought by

linguistic considerations, and particularly the fact that language itself has become the object of the autonomous and rapidly advancing science of linguistics, has altered this unhappy situation—or so it has seemed to many influential critics. Asked to justify his concern with literature and with talking about literature, the common reader was first assumed to need some sort of philosophical theory; the rise of science that threatened many literary men suggested to others that science could provide such a theory, but the sciences that were turned to proved to be not intimately enough connected with literature. Now, however, there is a highly respectable science that takes as its object of investigation language, the very stuff of which literature is made: wouldn't it seem reasonable to hope that at last the promised land is within view?

I myself don't think it is. Nor do I believe in the existence of such a promised land or, therefore, in the necessity of searching for it. Yet I also think that any serious reader of literature who does not trouble himself to find out why other, and equally serious, readers have felt the need of such beliefs is missing a great deal. In the following chapters, with both sorts of readers in mind, I try to show why I have come to believe as I do.

In my Preface I mentioned that my original reason for thinking general semantics might be a good point of departure for an introduction to an anthology of essays on language was simply the extraordinary influence that the writings of Korzybski and his followers have had on teachers of English; as I looked at general semantics more closely, I saw that there were at least two other reasons why it would be the right point of departure for the book my anthology had turned into. The first reason is that semantics is both ubiquitous and yet curiously elusive. Since considerations of meaning (as opposed, say, to phonological considerations) are of importance not only to the linguist but also to the philosopher of language, the literary critic, and the everyday user of words, most people automatically assume that semantic knowledge will be the kind of linguistic knowledge that will prove most useful to the nonspecialist. Consider how often, and in how many areas of discourse, people fall back on the fashionable pseudo-explanation that a particular problem or disagreement is "merely a matter of semantics." Yet while everybody talks about semantics, nobody (or almost nobody) does much about it: of all the fields of linguistic study, semantics is by far the least developed and therefore the most mysterious. The second reason is that general semantics is so very general: it is not only terribly ambitious in both its theoretical and its practical aims, it is also a great (and very convenient) omnium-gatherum of popular ideas about language. I therefore decided to use general semantics to bring to light, in my first chapter, the main concepts I wanted to use in later chapters to discuss the relations between linguistics, the philosophy of language, and literary criticism.

In my second chapter I set out to sketch the outlines of what I take to be a more promising semantic theory than Korzybski's, the theory that has grown out of the linguistic researches associated with the name of Noam Chomsky. But since the relation of Chomsky's transformational generative grammar to traditional American descriptive or structural linguistics is important, complex, and not very well known to the sort of common reader I was aiming at, I found I had to examine that relation at what may at first seem unnecessary length in order to make clear why I think the Chomskyan sort of semantics is more promising not only than general semantics but also than the semantics of descriptive linguists.

Finally, I wanted to argue in my last chapter that even the Chomskyan sort of semantics, though more promising in itself than the other sorts, is not directly relevant to literary criticism. But I also wanted to show that the reasons why this is so are not special ad hoc reasons having only to do with Chomskyan semantics but extremely powerful and general reasons. The best way to do this seemed to be to show first why attempts to make branches of linguistics other than semantics relevant to criticism have failed, and then to show that the most famous attempt to make another kind of semantics similarly relevant, the attempt embodied in the early work of I. A. Richards mentioned above, failed for the same reasons.

The synthesis I have attempted will thus appear to be not only limited but also rather negative—if indeed one can speak of a negative synthesis. But this need not be discouraging since experiments that turn out negatively are often as valuable as the other kind. To discover that a given chemical compound cannot be made to behave in a certain way is, after all, to discover something positive about its nature; similarly, to discover that (and why) attempts to make the scientific study of meaning (or of language in general) relevant to criticism have failed is to discover something positive, and I hope valuable, about the nature of criticism and therefore about the activity of the common reader.

semantics,
linguistics,
and
criticism

general
semantics
and the
science
of
meaning

The aim of general semantics is to improve our chances of survival by increasing our ability to understand and cooperate with one another. Of course this aim has been shared, particularly since 1945, by a great many people, and what sets general semanticists apart is the way they go about accomplishing it. Count Alfred Korzybski and his followers, the most important of whom are Stuart Chase and S. I. Hayakawa,[1] believe

---

[1] Alfred Korzybski's most important book, usually regarded as the Bible of general semantics, is *Science and Sanity: An Introduction to Non-aristotelian Systems and General Semantics* (Lancaster, Pa.: International Non-aristotelian Library, 1st ed., 1933, 4th ed., 1958. Distributed by Institute of General Semantics). The popularizations that have had most influence are Stuart Chase's *The Tyranny of Words* (New York: Harcourt Brace Jovanovich, 1938) and *The Power of Words* (New York: Har-

that most of our past misunderstandings—from break-fast-table squabbles right up to global wars—have resulted from the distorted view of reality which language, molding our thought in ways we are largely unaware of, has forced upon us. Language, they tell us, was devised to help us pool our knowledge and thus to give us a better chance of surviving in a difficult and often hostile world, but so far we have realized our capacities for cooperative enterprise only in the sciences, which avoid the pitfalls of ordinary language by using the special and superior language of mathematics. In other areas, where we must use ordinary language, our persistently irrational attitudes towards it have kept us little better than children or savages. With an urgency we can appreciate if we recall what was happening in 1933, Korzybski wrote:

> Since the World War certain conditions are becoming increasingly more difficult, and the infantile and animalistic systems drive us fatalistically toward further catastrophes. Whether these disasters will occur, the unknown future shall decide; but out of this unknown, one fact remains a certainty; namely, that this will depend on whether or not science can take hold of human affairs . . . [p. 549]

The urgency sharpened as the thirties drew to a close and Hayakawa wrote in 1939: "Linguistic naïveté —our tendency to think like savages about practically all subjects other than the purely technological—is not

---

court Brace Jovanovich, 1954); and S. I. Hayakawa's *Language in Action* (New York: Harcourt Brace Jovanovich, 1939) and its later revision *Language in Thought and Action* (New York: Harcourt Brace Jovanovich, 1949), which was itself revised in 1964. In giving references to *Science and Sanity*, I shall simply give the page number in parentheses; in references to the other books, the page number will be preceded by an abbreviation of the title: *TW, PW, LA,* and *LTA* respectively for the books listed above. I shall also refer to Hayakawa's recent collection of essays *Symbol, Status, and Personality* (New York: Harcourt Brace Jovanovich, 1963) as *SSP*. All references to *LTA* will be to the 1964 revision.

a factor to be ignored in trying to account for the mess civilization is in" *(LA, p. 36)*. And Chase had written a year earlier: "Confusions persist and increase because we have no true picture of the world outside, and so cannot talk to one another about how to stop them" *(TW, p. 352)*. To Korzybski it seemed that science would "take hold of human affairs" only if the study of meaning itself—of the relations between words, the world, and our "semantic reactions" —attained the status of an empirical science, and the construction of this new science was the task that he set himself.

Now *Science and Sanity* is an extremely forbidding book and is probably read nowadays by very few people—as Stuart Chase candidly admits, "A book on the clarification of meaning should not be so difficult to understand" *(TW, p. 94)*. But if we are to get a clear idea of general semantics, it is still to Korzybski rather than his popularizers that we must go, so I shall begin by simply paraphrasing his argument, using his own words wherever possible and withholding judgment until the picture is complete. This will enable me to avoid tiresomely repeating "Korzybski says" and "Korzybski tells us" and "Korzybski writes." Until I give further notice, then, what follows is to be taken not as my own view but as Korzybski's—or at least as what I understand his view to have been.

I

The first step in reaching a scientific understanding of the way language works is to make the following distinction between two levels—or groups of levels— of reality: first there is the objective or unspeakable or nonverbal level (or levels), composed of objects, events, and feelings as we experience them, and of the submicroscopic flux that lies behind these, inaccessible to ordinary sense experience but known to modern physics; then there is the verbal level (or levels), composed of the words and statements we use to talk about the objective level(s). This distinction is sharp and absolute, since

> . . . an object or feeling, say, our toothache, is *not* verbal, is *not* words. Whatever we may say will not be the objective level, which remains fundamentally un-speakable. Thus, we can sit on the object called "a chair," but we cannot sit on the noise we made or the name we applied to that object. . . . The objective level is *not* words, can *not* be reached by words alone. . . . *[p. 34]*

That is, we can say "toothache" or "chair," or we can make statements like "This is the ugliest chair I've ever seen" or "This is the third toothache I've had in two weeks"; but by using words alone we can never give another person the experience of seeing the chair, nor can we make him feel the pain in our tooth. Of course he can look at the chair for himself if he wants to (though it makes no sense even to imagine the possibility of his having somebody else's toothache), but the point is that we cannot *speak* either the chair or the toothache, we can only speak words.

Now this distinction seems obvious enough once it is pointed out, yet we habitually overlook it and confuse or identify verbal levels with objective levels. And the structure of our language encourages such confusions:

> Thus, for instance, we *handle* what we call a pencil. Whatever we *handle* is un-speakable; yet we *say* "this *is* a pencil," which statement is unconditionally false to facts, because the object appears as an absolute individual and *is not* words. . . . "Say whatever you choose *about* the object, and whatever you might say *is not* it." Or, in other words: "Whatever you might *say* the object 'is,' well it *is not*." *[p. 35]*

Statements like "This is a pencil," which assert that something *is* something else and which we may call subject-predicate statements, are fundamental to languages like English, and their importance is augmented by the fact that the logic we have inherited from Aristotle "assumed that everything could be expressed in a subject-predicate form" *(p. 189)*. Yet such statements, simply by virtue of their form, invariably assert something false. This point will become clear if we first understand that in all ordinary perception our nervous systems mislead us in a way analogous to the way language misleads us.

"If we take something, anything, let us say the object already referred to, called 'pencil,' and enquire what it represents, according to science 1933, we find that the 'scientific object' represents an 'event,' a mad dance of 'electrons,' which is different every instant, which never repeats itself, which is known to consist of extremely complex dynamic processes of very fine structure, acted upon by, and reacting upon, the rest of the universe, inextricably connected with everything else and dependent on everything else" *(p. 387)*. Thus the pencil as we see it, an ordinary object that seems stable and self-contained, is an illusion: the reality is a submicroscopic event that "our rough 'senses' " *(p. 383)* are "not adapted to register" *(p. 382)*. It is the same with all ordinary objects: each is really "only a shadow cast by the scientific object" *(p. 402)*, and "we *see* what we see because we *miss* all the finer details" *(p. 376)*. Therefore, "if we enquire as to the neurological processes involved in registering the object, we find that the nervous system has *abstracted,* from the infinite numbers of sub-microscopic characteristics of the event, a large but finite number of macroscopic characteristics" *(pp. 387–389)*, and so we may think of the ordinary object as an *abstraction* from the scientific object or event.

We see then that the relation between the two nonverbal levels of reality is such that the second level (the ordinary object) is an abstraction constructed from the first by omitting "all the finer details" –

though in practice we usually confuse the two levels and imagine that the pencil we see is the pencil that is really "out there" in the world. The relation between the second nonverbal level and the first verbal level— between, that is, the ordinary object and the name or label we attach to it—is precisely the same, for "the number of characteristics which we ascribe by *definition* to the label is still smaller than the number of characteristics the [ordinary] object has" *(p. 387)*. Even if we gave a favorite pencil a proper name (as people give names to their boats or cars) rather than simply calling it "pencil," "we would ascribe, perhaps, its length, thickness, shape, colour, hardness, etc.[2] But we would mostly *disregard* the accidental characteristics, such as a scratch on its surface, or the kind of glue by which the two wooden parts of the objective 'pencil' are held together, etc." *(p. 387)*. Thus "we see that the object *is not* the event but an abstraction from it, and that the label *is not* the object nor the event, but a still further abstraction" *(p. 389)*. Yet just as we usually confuse the scientific object with the ordinary object, so too we usually confuse the ordinary object with the label we attach to it. That we do so is largely a result of the subject-predicate structure of our language, as seen in statements like "This is a pencil"—to which we are now ready to return.

Now "all language can be considered as names either for un-speakable entities on the objective level, be it things or feelings, or as *names for relations*" *(p. 20)*. It is important to notice that some words are names for relations rather than for objects, because it is this fact that keeps a sentence or statement from being a mere list. "When we use a series of names for objects, 'Smith, Brown, Jones' etc., we say *nothing*. We do not produce a proposition. But if we say 'Smith kicks

[2] "Etc." is one—the first one we have encountered—of a number of expressions Korzybski habitually abbreviates, as he explains on pp. 15–16. Here and subsequently I have tacitly expanded these abbreviations.

Brown,' we have introduced the term 'kicks,' which is not a name for an object, but . . . a 'relation word' " *(p. 152)*. By analogy, we can see that in "This is a pencil," "this" and "pencil" are names for objects and "is" is the name of a relation asserted to hold between them, the relation we usually call identity or " 'absolute sameness' in *'all'* aspects *(p. 941)*. But since "whatever we can see, handle etc., represents an *absolute individual,* and *different from anything else"* *(p. 262)*, it is clear that identity is "never to be found in this world, nor in our heads" *(p. 194)*, and that therefore all assertions of identity are "structurally false to fact" *(p. 202)*. So the statement "This is a pencil" misleads us by asserting a nonexistent relation. But it also misleads us in another way, more directly related to the distinction between verbal and objective levels from which we began. "This" refers to a particular pencil as we experience it, a second level nonverbal abstraction, while "pencil" refers to a verbal abstraction, the set of defining characteristics common to all pencils. Therefore "This is a pencil" not only confuses two separate entities by asserting them to be identical, but also confuses nonverbal with verbal reality because the two entities it asserts to be identical exist on different sides of the line that separates one group of levels from the other.

This double confusion is characteristic of subject-predicate statements, and so it is clear that the subject-predicate structure of our language encourages us to think of the relation between language and nonverbal reality as one of identity. But what is the true relation? We have seen that just as every ordinary object of experience is an abstraction from a submicroscopic event, so any label we attach to the ordinary object is an abstraction from *it.* And we have also seen that a similar relation holds between true statements and facts—taking facts to be collections of ordinary objects in some relation to one another. That is, "Smith kicks Brown" is true (if it is true) because the object desig-

nated by "Smith" happens to be in the relation designated by "kicks" to the object designated by "Brown."
And "This is a pencil" is (and must necessarily be)
always false because the relation designated by "is"
could never possibly hold between any two entities—
even if they existed on the same side of the verbal-
nonverbal dividing line, as Smith and Brown do. To
put it another way: that Smith kicks Brown can be a
fact and is at least a possible state of affairs, but that
this is a pencil can never even be a possible state of
affairs, let alone a fact.

Thus we can say that a true statement must fit or
correspond to some fact, for though the statement will
inevitably omit "all the finer details" of the fact it
represents, it must at least have a *structure* similar to
that of the fact—it won't do to say "Brown kicks
Smith" if Smith is kicking Brown. The relation of a
true statement to a fact—and, by extension, of a statement that might sometimes be true to a possible state
of affairs—will then be rather like the relation of an
accurate map to its piece of territory, for "a map *is not*
the territory it represents, but, if correct, it has a *similar structure* to the territory, which accounts for its
usefulness" *(p. 58)*. When we generalize this insight
about statements to language as a whole, we see that
"as words *are not* the objects which they represent,
structure, and structure alone, becomes the only link
which connects our verbal processes with the empirical
data" *(p. 59)*. Therefore "if we reflect upon our languages, we find that at best they must be considered
only as maps" *(p. 58)*.

Now "any map or language, to be of maximum
usefulness, should, in structure, be similar to the
structure of the empirical world. Likewise, from
the point of view of a theory of sanity, any system
or language should, in structure, be similar to the
structure of our nervous system" *(p. 11)*. If a language does not fulfill these conditions, the consequences for its speakers can be disastrous. "We do

not realize what tremendous power the structure of an habitual language has. It is not an exaggeration to say that it enslaves us . . . and that the structure which a language exhibits, and impresses upon us unconsciously, is *automatically projected* upon the world around us" *(p. 90)*. In the past "the usual procedure" has been as follows: "first, we have our structurally 'preconceived' doctrines and languages; next, we observe the structure of the world; and *then* we try to force the observed facts into the linguistic structural patterns" *(p. 219)*. Obviously this won't do, and in fact "our only possible procedure in advancing our knowledge" is to do exactly the reverse, "to match our verbal structures, often called theories, with empirical structures, and see if our verbal predictions are fulfilled empirically or not, thus indicating that the two structures are either similar or dissimilar" *(p. 63)*. Therefore we must *"start* with silent observations, and search empirically for structure; next, we invent verbal structures similar to them; and, finally, we see what can be said about the situation, and so test the language" *(p. 219)*.

So the task that lies before us is nothing less than to revise the structure of our language, and it will involve asking (and, if possible, answering) three very large questions, the first and third of which we have already answered in part. (1) What are the structures of the empirical world and of the nervous system? (2) What language (if any) has a structure that matches their structures, and how does it do this? (3) What (if anything) can be done to bring the structure of English closer to that of the ideal language?

We have already seen that "whatever we can see, handle etc., represents an *absolute individual,* and *different from anything else" (p. 262),* so we can say that "in general terms, the structure of the external world is such that we deal always on the objective levels with absolute individuals, with absolute differences" *(p. 263)*. But "in a world of only absolute differences, without similarities, recognition, and, therefore, 'intelligence,' would be impossible" *(p. 165)*. Intelligence is only made possible by the nervous system, which possesses a structure that enables us to recognize similarities as well as differences. This structure "is such that, on some levels, we produce dynamic abstractions; on others, static" *(p. 288)*. The dynamic abstractions (which we ordinarily call sensations) are "manufactured by the lower nerve centres, which are closer to, and in direct contact with, actual life experiences" *(p. 297)*. Since "the outside world is an everchanging chain of events, a kind of flux; . . . those nerve centres in closest contact with the outside world must react in a shifting way" *(p. 290)*, and so the dynamic abstractions they manufacture are "non-permanent, shifting, vague and un-speakable, . . . cannot be transmitted, . . . and have a private, non-public character" *(p. 297)*. "As 'sensations' were often very deceptive and, therefore, did not always lead to survival, a nervous system which somehow retained vestiges, or 'memories,' of former 'sensations' and could recombine them, shift them etc., proved of higher survival value, and so 'intelligence' evolved, from the lowest to the highest degrees" *(p. 169)*. These vestiges or memories (which we ordinarily call ideas or mental images) are "abstractions from the lower order abstractions" *(p. 297)* that we call sensations, and since "they have *lost* their *shifting* character" *(p. 291)* by virtue of "being further removed from the outside world" *(p. 297)*, they are "relatively static" *(p. 291)*, "capable of being transmitted" *(p. 280)*, and "may be preserved and used over and over again in extra-neural forms, as recorded in books and otherwise" *(p. 291)*. In fact the "main importance" of these static abstractions "is in their *public* character" *(p. 280)*. We can say then that "the nervous system is an abstracting, integrating mechanism" *(p. 310)* whose "structure . . . is such that it abstracts, or generalizes, or integrates etc., in higher orders, and so finds similarities" *(p. 263)*.

Now we are in a position to ask our second question, whether any known language has a structure that matches those of the empirical world and the nervous system. Since "we deal always on the objective levels with absolute individuals, with absolute differences" *(p. 263)*, it is obvious that any language whose structure was to match that of the empirical world would have to contain "an indefinite number of *proper names, each different*" *(262)*; but if its structure were also to match that of the nervous system, it would also have to contain static, higher order abstractions that would make it possible to show similarities as well as differences. When we reflect that "mathematizing [has] proved to be *at each historical period* the most excellent human activity, producing results of such enormous importance and unexpected validity as not to be compared with any other musings of man" *(p. 67)*, mathematics would seem the most likely candidate for our ideal language. And sure enough, when we examine the structure of mathematics this hunch is borne out and the reasons for its superiority as a language become clear.

Since English (like all other natural languages) contains only a finite number of words, it obviously fails to meet our first requirement, that the ideal language contain "an indefinite number of *proper names, each different*" *(p. 262)*. But when we turn to mathematics, "we find such a language *uniquely* in numbers, each number 1, 2, 3 etc., being a unique, sharply distinguishable, *proper name*" *(p. 262)*. At first glance English does seem to meet our second requirement, since words like "pencil" are static, higher order abstractions that indicate the ways in which all pencils are similar to each other. But when we look more closely, we see that everyday abstractions like "pencil" are defective in a way that mathematical abstractions like "circle" are not, for "we may describe or 'define' a 'pencil' in as great detail as we please, yet it is impossible to include *all* the characteristics which we may discover in this actual objective pencil" *(p. 68)*. This, as we saw, is one of the reasons subject-predicate statements are always false. But "in our definition of a mathematical circle" as "the locus of all points in a plane at equal distance from a point called the centre," it is clear that

> . . . *all particulars* [are] included, and whatever we may find about this mathematical circle later on will be strictly dependent on this definition, and no new characteristics, not already included in the definition, will ever appear. We see, here, that *mathematical abstractions are characterized by the fact that they have all particulars included.* [p. 67]

Combining our two requirements, we might say that what we need, and what English fails on two counts to provide, is a kind of proper name that will show differences and similarities simultaneously. Now the vocabulary of mathematics contains not only numerical constants like 1 and 2 that can function just as proper names like "Smith" and "Brown" do in English, but also variables like x and y. Therefore we can create expressions like

> . . . x_i, $(i = 1, 2, 3, \ldots n)$, where the x shows, let us say, that we deal with a variable x with many values, and the number we assign to i indicates the individuality under consideration. From the structural point of view, such a vocabulary is similar to the world around us; it accounts for the individuality of the external objects, it also is similar to the structure of our nervous system, because it allows generalizations or higher order abstractions, emphasizes the abstracting nervous characteristics, etc. The subscript emphasizes the differences; the letter x implies the similarities. [p. 262]

Therefore expressions of the form x_i are the sort of proper name we are looking for.

So much for our second question. But if we are to

find an answer to our third, we must find some way of creating expressions like x_i in ordinary English, of manufacturing "an endless array of individual names without unduly expanding the vocabulary" *(p. 381)*. As it happens, this can be done, for "in daily language a similar device is extremely useful and has very far-reaching psycho-logical semantic effects. Thus, if we say 'pencil$_1$,' 'pencil$_2$,' . . . pencil$_n$' " *(p. 263)*, we "produce individual names, and so cover the *differences*" among individual pencils, and also, "by keeping the main root word 'pencil,' we keep the implications of daily life, and also of *similarities*" *(p. 381)*. Therefore the first major way in which we can revise the structure of English is to append index numbers like 1 and 2 to general terms like "pencil." "It has already been emphasized repeatedly that our abstracting from physical objects or situations proceeds by missing, neglecting, or forgetting" characteristics, and it is precisely

. . . those disregarded characteristics [that] usually produce errors in evaluation, resulting in the disasters of life. If we acquire this extensional mathematical habit of using special names for unique individuals, we become conscious, not only of the similarities, but also of the differences, which consciousness is one of the mechanisms for helping the proper evaluation and so preventing or eliminating semantic disturbances. *[pp. 381–382]*

This consciousness, which we may call consciousness of abstracting, may be defined as an *"awareness* that in our process of abstracting we have *left out* characteristics" *(p. 416)*. Now we saw earlier that subject-predicate statements like "This is a pencil," by asserting the nonexistent relation of identity to hold between the particular pencil before us and the label "pencil," work against the achievement of this awareness by encouraging us to forget that the process of abstracting by which we have constructed the label from the object involved the omission of some of the object's characteristics. Since the trouble-maker in such statements (and in languages like English which are based on them) is the seemingly innocent word "is," we may also define consciousness of abstracting as "remembering the *'is not'* " *(p. 416)* that lies behind every "is." The achievement of this consciousness will then also be seen to depend on "the denial of the 'is' of identity" *(p. 417)*—that is, on never using "is" as it is used in subject-predicate statements. This is the second major revision we must make in the structure of English. "If we use the 'is' at all, and it is extremely difficult to avoid entirely this auxiliary verb when using languages which, to a large extent, depend on it, we must be particularly careful not to use 'is' as an identity term" *(p. 400)*.

Therefore the two main answers to our third question are that we should use index numbers and avoid the "is" of identity. But since "the introduction of a few new, and the rejection of some old, terms suggests desirable structural changes" *(p. 59)*, it will also help if we use terms like "order," "relation," "structure," and "space-time," and avoid terms like "space" and "time," which are false to the world as we know it through modern physics and as misleading in their way as "is." If we make these revisions, "the new desirable semantic results [will] follow as *automatically* as the old undesirable ones followed" *(p. 63)* from the use of the old, primitive subject-predicate language.

II

This is the basic argument of *Science and Sanity,* and we may turn now to consider its merits. If we revise our language in the ways Korzybski recommends, will the resulting consciousness of abstracting actually give us a clearer view of the world and make us able to agree and cooperate with one another more often than we do now? Perhaps the first thing that strikes us is that Korzybski and his disciples, in their books, don't use the revised language but just ordinary English. They rarely employ index numbers except when telling us that we should, and one doesn't get the impression that they use "is" any differently, or any less often, than other writers. Of course this might just be because they are writing for an audience that still speaks and reads the old, unrevised sort of English: once Korzybski's ideas have been put into practice on a grand scale, not only general semantics texts but all books will be peppered with index numbers and all writers will use "is," as Hayakawa recommends, only "as an auxiliary verb ('he is coming')" *(LTA, p. 315)*. But I shall argue that this is not the real reason. I think the real reason lies deeper, in the fact that Korzybski's recommendations spring from a general view of the nature and origin of language that is about as mistaken as it could possibly be; they have not been followed, even by their originator, simply because they cannot be.

Take the index numbers first. What if I suddenly began writing sentences like "Semanticist$_3$ writes in book$_7$ that philosopher$_{12}$ wrongly answers question$_{38}$" instead of "Chase writes in *The Tyranny of Words* that Plato wrongly answers the question of what words mean"? I take it this is the sort of sentence that Korzybski's recommendation, followed as literally and generally as he wants it to be, would produce. At any rate the problem is clear: how would you know (for example) which semanticist I was assigning the index number 3 to, unless we had previously agreed on it? Of course if I were speaking rather than writing and if Chase happened to be in the room, I could point to him as I said "semanticist$_3$," but I couldn't very well point to Plato without digging him up, and questions like "the question of what words mean" are not even objects and so cannot even be dug up and pointed to.

Some previous agreement would therefore be necessary. But agreements can only be made in language and it is important to ask which language we would use to make these, ordinary English or the new revised language employing index numbers. If we reflect a moment, it seems clear that to say things like "Let Plato be philosopher$_{12}$" or "Let the question of what words mean be question$_{38}$" we need the proper names, general terms, and individuating descriptive phrases of ordinary English. To try to use only the new language would be like trying to give somebody the key to a code in a message written in that code: if he already knew the code there would be no point in giving him the key, and if he didn't know it then he wouldn't understand the message. So whenever we wanted to talk about a new semanticist or question or anything else that was not there to be pointed to, we would have to drop back into ordinary English. There could never be a point at which even two people (let alone a whole linguistic community) could agree to use only the new revised language simply because there is never a point at which anybody can enumerate and classify in advance all the things he is going to want to talk about in the future.

Since we could never adopt the new language and stick to it, the index numbers could never contribute to a general linguistic revision in the way Korzybski hoped. At best they would be like code words or abbreviations that we adopt for reasons of secrecy or convenience, explain at the time of their adoption, and use within the context of our ordinary language. For example: "From now on, in the interests of national security, all official communiqués will refer to the pending invasion of Canada as OPERATION TUNDRA." Perhaps Hayakawa unconsciously realizes this, for he reduces the index numbers still further, to private mnemonic devices, and waters down Korzybski's recommendation to the advice that we "Use *index numbers* and *dates* as reminders that *no word ever has exactly the same meaning twice.* Cow$_1$ is *not* cow$_2$, cow$_2$ is *not* cow$_3$, . . . Smith$_{1963}$ is *not* Smith$_{1964}$,

Smith$_{1965}$ is *not* Smith$_{1970}$, . . ." *(LTA, p. 315).* If the index numbers are merely private "reminders," the troubling question of prior agreement is sidestepped since there is no one else to agree with; and it is also sidestepped by thinking of dates as examples of index numbers since we have already agreed which year was 1965 and which was 1970. But of course to treat the index numbers as Hayakawa does is to give up the effort to make English structurally similiar to mathematics, and thus tacitly to admit that one of Korzybski's central aims is mistaken.

Korzybski and his followers obviously sense the practical difficulties involved in using index numbers since they don't use them themselves, and we might well wonder how they could have missed the important theoretical difficulty we have noticed. I think the reason is that they, like many earlier thinkers, believe quite seriously that language itself was instituted among men by just the sort of impossible agreement—or "convention," as it has often been called—that the assigning of the index numbers would demand. This can be seen in Korzybski but it comes through still more clearly in Chase and Hayakawa. They are more practical and less theoretical than he is, and since agreement is the main practical result that his theories are supposed to produce, they are eager to show that we have a heritage of agreement dating back to the very establishment of the most characteristically human institution. As an example take Hayakawa's definition of "the symbolic process":

> The process by means of which human beings can arbitrarily make certain things *stand for* other things may be called the *symbolic process.* Whenever two or more human beings can communicate with each other, they can, by agreement, make anything stand for anything. . . .
>
> Of all forms of symbolism, language is the most highly developed, most subtle, and most complicated. It has been pointed out that human beings, by agreement, can make anything stand for anything. Now, human beings have agreed, in the course of

centuries of mutual dependency, to let the various noises that they can produce with their lungs, throats, tongues, teeth, and lips systematically stand for specified happenings in their nervous systems. We call that system of agreements *language*. [LTA, pp. 24, 26–27]

Or take this little fable Chase tells to help us remember that "words have no meaning in themselves":

> Suppose that an Englishman and a Frenchman are wrecked on a desert island. . . . Each flatly refuses to learn the other's language. . . . Gestures serve for a time, but for certain tasks words are badly needed. So they decide, by gestures, to invent a new language which is neither French nor English. . . .
>
> They go down to the beach and begin. John points to the sea, waving his arm to comprehend the whole expanse. Louis nods. John writes on his pad WAM. Louis nods. "Wam" is to be the word for "sea" and "mer." . . . And so they go round the island, making up strictly neutral words, short and easy, for all the common objects in which they are mutually interested because of the work there is to do. Then John invites Louis by gestures to look at him while he does a pantomime walk. "Rab" is the word for walk, "ral" that for run. . . . So they invent words for all their common acts.
>
> Now the task becomes more difficult. They have a word for "tree," but how shall they signify a collection of trees, or a wood? They work it out, perhaps by adding "ez" as a suffix. With this symbolic outfit, . . . their daily labors of fishing, foodgetting, cooking, shelter-building, are greatly aided. *Yet not a single word means anything in itself.* [TW, pp. 71–72]

Now it is not hard to see why the idea that language was instituted by agreement has appealed even to men who, unlike general semanticists, have had no special stake in proving that "Cultural and intellectual cooperation is the great principle of *human* life" (*LTA, p. 14*). If history had been a bit different, after all, we might well be saying "electropix" instead of "television" or —as one Renaissance logician actually proposed— "endsay" instead of "conclusion"; and we know as a matter of record that we say "anode," "cathode," and "ion" merely because a nineteenth-century polymath named Whewell happened to suggest the terms to Faraday. It is easy enough, then, to imagine that any object or quality or action might have been called something different, and of course in foreign languages almost all of them are. "Thus we may conceive," wrote Locke, "how *words* . . . came to be made use of by men as the signs of their ideas; not by any natural connexion that there is between particular articulate sounds and certain ideas, for then there would be but one language amongst all men; but by a voluntary imposition, whereby such a word is made arbitrarily the mark of such an idea."[3]

But we forsake the realm of possibility for the kingdom of myth when we extrapolate from the picture of civilized men agreeing, in a common language they already speak, to call television "television," to the picture of languageless men somehow conveying to each other by gestures the revolutionary idea of instituting a language with a certain grammar, sound system, and vocabulary. As Bertrand Russell once remarked, "We can hardly suppose a parliament of hitherto speechless elders meeting together and agreeing to call a cow a cow and a wolf a wolf."[4] Yet this is precisely what Hayakawa and Chase do suppose in the passages just quoted. Though Chase admits that grammatical inflections might be "more difficult" to agree on than names, he does not realize that pointing is not necessarily a clear and unambiguous way of singling out features of the physical world for attention and that therefore it might be impossible even to agree on names: "Words, unlike pointing, have no meaning in themselves" *(TW, p. 54)*, he tells us, clearly implying that acts of pointing do have meaning in themselves. But what if, when John pointed to the sea, Louis thought he was trying to elicit a word for water or

[3] *Essay Concerning Human Understanding*, III, ii, 1.

[4] *The Analysis of Mind* (London: Allen and Unwin, 1921), p. 190.

wave or blue or deep or wide? Or what if Louis did not even see that John's object was to get him to agree on a word? Such misunderstandings could not possibly be prevented or cleared up without a common language already being in use. Hayakawa seems in fact to realize this when he qualifies his definition of the symbolic process by adding "Whenever two or more human beings can communicate with each other." But then a few pages later, when he comes to apply the definition specifically to language, he omits the qualification: "It has been pointed out that human beings, by agreement, can make anything stand for anything."

So the conventionalist myth (as it is sometimes called) assumes precisely what it sets out to explain, the existence of a common language; and once we see through the myth, we can also see through Korzybski's recommendation about index numbers. Let us turn now to his recommendation that we "abandon permanently the use of the 'is' of identity" (p. 60), a recommendation based, we recall, on his conviction that what he calls subject-predicate statements are really identity statements that inevitably assert something false about a world in which nothing is exactly like anything else and everything is in perpetual flux. Since this view of subject-predicate statements is the main source of the opposition to Aristotle that led Korzybski to christen his own system "non-aristotelian," it is at least as important to him as his belief that ordinary English can and must be made structurally similar to mathematics. And it is just as vulnerable. In the first place, as Max Black has pointed out, Korzybski is charging Aristotle not merely with an absurdity but with an absurdity that Aristotle expressly repudiated:

What Aristotle is alleged to have believed and taught is that such statements as "Water is wet" and "Dewey is a philosopher" mean that water is *identical* with wetness, and Dewey is *identical* with the characteristic of being a philosopher. . . .

It is worth noting that Korzybski gives no quotation from Aristotle to support this charge. And it should be said, as a matter of historical justice, that there is no evidence that Aristotle or his followers believed anything so absurd. One sufficient reason is that the view with which they are charged would be inconsistent with the standard syllogistic doctrine of the impossibility of converting universal propositions. If the "is" in "Water is wet" were the "is" of identity, as alleged, the truth of that proposition would automatically entail the truth of the converse proposition that all wetness is water. Now it is, of course, a central part of the doctrine of Aristotelian logic that the proposition *All A is B* can*not* be automatically replaced by the converse, *All B is A*. Again, if Aristotle believed the absurd doctrine which is ascribed to him, he would have to believe that Plato and Socrates and Aristotle himself were all the same person. For, if all of them were *identical* with being a philosopher, all of them must be identical with one another. Even a stupid man would hardly believe in these absurd consequences; and Aristotle was very far from being stupid.[5]

To this I might add that though there is a Greek word that behaves very much like our word "is," it can, unlike "is," often be omitted without damaging the sense of the sentence, and Aristotle often does omit it from subject-predicate propositions. More important, in the technical works outlining his theory of the syllogism Aristotle never uses this word in stating subject-predicate propositions, but in the interests of grammatical clarity replaces it either by a word that means "belongs to" or by one that means "is predicated of."

So Korzybski is wrong on two counts about subject-predicate propositions as they appear in Aristotelian

[5] "Korzybski's General Semantics," in *Language and Philosophy* (Ithaca, N.Y.: Cornell University Press, 1949), p. 230. Korzybski's misconceptions about logic in general and Aristotelian logic in particular are the part of his work I am least qualified to deal with; I am therefore especially grateful to Professor Black for covering them thoroughly in his excellent essay.

logic: they are not assertions of identity and they need not (and usually do not) contain an "is." Therefore his recommendation is pointless since it was made to correct a situation that does not exist, and we can see it is absurd as well if we simply try not using "is" for a while. It won't do merely to say that "it is extremely difficult to avoid entirely this auxiliary verb when using languages which, to a large extent, depend on it" *(p. 400):* we must realize that it is impossible to do so and still speak English. But as with the index numbers, the interesting thing is not the absurdity of Korzybski's recommendation but the reasons he and his followers don't see that it's absurd—reasons that again have to do with a mistaken general view of the origin of language.

In specifying the sort of identity that subject-predicate statements assert, Korzybski often speaks of a language founded on such statements and on the "is" of identity as "a language of 'sensations' " *(e.g., p. 372).* To show the unreliability of such a language he gives this example:

Let us take three pails of water; the first at the temperature of 10° centigrade, the second at 30°, and the third at 50°. Let us put the left hand in the first pail and the right in the third. If we presently withdraw the left hand from the first pail and put it in the second, we feel how nicely *warm* the water in the second pail is. But, if we withdraw the right hand from the third pail and put it in the second, we notice how *cold* the water is. The temperature of the water in the second pail was practically not different in the two cases, yet our feelings registered a marked difference. The difference in the "feel" depended on the former conditions to which our hands had been subjected. Thus, we see that a language of "senses" is not a very reliable language, and that we cannot depend on it for general purposes of evaluation. *[pp. 372–373]*

Now no one would quarrel with some of the implications we are meant to draw from this. Feelings may indeed vary from one person to another, and the same person's may vary under varying conditions. It would be stupid to forget or ignore this, and to insist that because the water felt warm it simply *was* warm and that anybody who said it was (or felt) cold either was not feeling it properly or had damaged nerve-endings. Moreover, we perhaps can agree that "This water is warm," by virtue of its subject-predicate form, does have a flatly assertive quality that minimizes the degree to which what we say about the water depends on variable conditions, and that it suggests that the water's warmth is a more or less durable attribute people would no more disagree about than they would about the roundness of a clock's face. Certainly we can more easily imagine such a disagreement arising about the water than about the clock, and while there would be ways of determining whether or not the clock's face was round, it is hard to know what it would mean to determine whether the water was warm or cold. Of course we could always measure its temperature, but that is not what is at issue. In the event of a disagreement, we might want to revise "This water is warm" to "This water *feels* warm to me": this would show our realization that it might feel cold to somebody else and that it would be point-less (and even meaningless) to go on arguing about whether it was *really* warm or *really* cold.

So much for the truth that Korzybski is apparently trying to bring out in his account of the statement. But it is important to notice that his way of putting it is different from the way I have put it above. He thinks that "This water is warm" only pretends to be about the water and is really a report of a sensation or feeling, but that the subject-predicate form of the statement makes its speaker unable to see this and tricks him into literally "identifying" his sensation with something in the outside world, into "projecting" it outside of himself and imagining that the water possesses some inherent, objective warmth or coldness. Korzybski thinks this kind of projection is very dangerous. "The so-called 'mentally' ill . . . project their own feelings, moods, and other structural implications on the outside world," he tells us, "and so build up delusions, illusions, and hallucinations, believing that what is going on *in* them is going on *outside* of them" *(p. 80).* But is this really a danger inherent in the form of the statement? Only for certain sorts of naïve amateur philosophers, it seems to me. For while an ordinary person not in the grasp of a theory might well be ignorant of a difference in conditions that would make the water feel cold to somebody else though it felt warm to him, and might pigheadedly insist that it just *was* warm because it felt warm, that would be quite different from insisting that the world was peopled with strange entities like Warmth and (as Korzybski often puts it) that the water had Warmth "added" to it—that its warmth existed as a discoverable part of it. General semanticists seem wholly unaware of this difference and far too ready to commit the ordinary person to foolish theories most of us would not dream of holding. And surely Korzybski is overstating his case when he says that "This water is warm" does not really say anything about the water but is merely a report of something "going on" inside the person who speaks it, of an effect caused in him by the water.

Yet one of his main justifications for abolishing the "is" of identity is his conviction that all subject-predicate statements are to be treated on this model, as leading inevitably to "projection" because they are really about feelings, even though they pretend to be about external objects. He asserts, for example, that "This blade of grass is green" is false in exactly the same way as "This water is warm":

If we carry [our analysis] far enough, we shall discover a very intricate, yet definite, relation or complex of relations between the objective blade of grass and the observer. Rays of light impinge upon the blade, are reflected from it, fall on the retina of our eye, and produce within our skins the feeling of "green" etc., an extremely complex process which has some definite structure. *[p. 62]*

Again we can agree that it would be stupid to think the statement implied an inherent "greenness" possessing "some sort of objective independence" *(p. 198)*, though again the temptation to do so does not seem worth worrying about. And again there might be situations in which we should instead want to say "This blade of grass looks green to me." But the differences between the two examples are really more important than the similarities. Whatever "unreliability" the statement "This water is warm" may be admitted to possess arises, as we saw, from the fact that the form of the statement makes the question of whether the water is warm or cold appear straightforwardly resolvable, whereas there is actually something oddly "subjective" about the way we apply words like "warm" and "cold." Now the way something looks, like the way it feels to the touch, does depend on certain variable conditions. But from this it does not follow that color words like "green" have the same air of subjectivity that words like "warm" and "cold" have. Of course people sometimes do disagree about the color of an object, but except for irrelevant borderline disputes of the sort that often arise with (for example) blue-green, it makes far more sense to speak of settling a disagreement about the color of an object than it does to speak of determining whether the water is really warm or cold. The move from "This water is warm" to "This water feels warm to me" is an admission that the disagreement is irresolvable, a standoff; but the move from "This blade of grass is green" to "This blade of grass looks green to me" is something else altogether. For to say that something looks green is to say that it looks the way something that really is green looks to somebody who has normal color vision and is in a position to see it properly, and to do this is not to admit that the matter cannot be resolved but rather to make an explicit appeal to the standards required to resolve it. We think of one set of conditions for seeing colors and applying color words as typical or standard, but are more flexible in applying words like "warm" and "cold"; this is why it would seem unnatural to invoke words like "normal" and "properly" in the case of the water, while it seems perfectly natural to do so with the blade of grass.[6]

So the grain of truth in Korzybski's overstated contention that "This water is warm" is an "unreliable" statement because it is really about something going on inside the speaker while it purports to be about something outside of him, is that the statement, and its revised version, do not make a particularly strong appeal to any set of standard conditions. When he is dealing with statements like "This blade of grass is green" or "This blade of grass looks green to me," which do make such an appeal, even this grain of truth vanishes. Furthermore, while it is not strictly accurate to say that either of the statements about the water is simply about a feeling or sensation, yet we do speak (loosely) of a "feeling of warmth" as though it were something going on inside us exactly in the sense that a pain or a feeling of nausea is, but we never speak, as Korzybski does, of "the feeling of 'green'" or of "a feeling which we express by saying, 'grass is green'" (p. 253). What is this feeling? Is it localized the way a pain is or not localized, the way feelings of sadness or elation are? Does it only come when we see something green or can we induce it by thinking of green objects? If there were such a feeling, questions like these would be perfectly legitimate ones

[6] Throughout this discussion I am indebted to Chapter VII of Gilbert Ryle's book *The Concept of Mind* (London: Hutchinson, 1949) and also to his essay "Sensation," most readily available in Robert J. Swartz (ed.), *Perceiving, Sensing, and Knowing* (Garden City, N.Y.: Anchor Books, 1965), pp. 187–203.

to ask. Yet the more of them we ask, the more absurd appears the contention that there is any such feeling. Green may of course have special feelings associated with it: it may evoke the smell of the Maine woods or make us sad about the loss of a loved one whose favorite color it was. But then again it may not, and anyway experiencing such feelings is not what we mean by seeing (something) green.

But of course Korzybski's talk—vague as it is—about light rays and "an extremely complex process" of "some definite structure" makes it clear that such familiar associated feelings are not what he has in mind. He is thinking rather of bodily processes which can be observed and described by neurologists and physiologists, and his assumption seems to be that there is a running correlation between these processes and our visual experience such that scientific descriptions of the processes will always say more precisely the same things we say when we say what color something is or appears to be. But it is very misleading to speak of such bodily processes as feelings or sensations since we simply are not aware of them—we don't experience or "have" them any more than we experience the "extremely complex process" that carries blood to the lungs. And it is simply a mistake (though a familiar one) to think that any statement about light rays or retinal images or the stimulation of nerve-endings will state—and state more precisely—the same fact stated by "This blade of grass is (or looks) green." It is more accurate to say that such technical statements offer *explanations* of some of the phenomena involved in the sort of situation in which the everyday statement is ordinarily used—and of course to do this involves stating quite different facts from the one stated by the everyday statement. Advances in physics and neurology over the past two hundred years have taught us a great deal about color and color vision, but they have not given the English sentence "This blade of grass is green" a meaning different from the one it had in the eighteenth century.

The disadvantages of Korzybski's ways of dealing with subject-predicate statements come out still more clearly in the following example:

How about the term "dog"? The number of individuals with which any one is directly acquainted is, by necessity, limited, and usually is small. Let us imagine that someone had dealt only with good-natured "dogs," and had never been bitten by any of them. Next he sees some animal; he says, "This *is* a dog"; his associations (relations) do not suggest a bite; he approaches the animal and begins to play with him, and is bitten. Was the statement "this *is* a dog" a safe statement? Obviously not. He approached the animal with semantic expectations and *evaluation* of his verbal definition, but was bitten by the non-verbal, un-speakable objective level, which has different characteristics. [*p. 373*]

Yet despite its obvious problems, "This (it) is a dog" is the statement Korzybski chooses to use in the bit of conjectural history he brings forward to justify speaking of a subject-predicate language as "a language of 'sensations' ":

When our primitive ancestors were building their language, . . . they identified their feelings with the outside world . . . If [they] saw an animal and called it "dog" and saw another animal roughly resembling the first, [they] said, quite happily, "it *is* a dog," forgetting or not knowing that the objective level is un-speakable and that we deal only with absolute individuals, each one different from the other. [*p. 372*]

Moreover, this sort of subject-predicate statement, in which the "is" is followed not by an adjective but by the indefinite article and a common noun, is the sort general semanticists most often use in showing us how to avoid "confusing levels of abstraction—confusing what is inside our heads with what is outside" (*LTA, p. 200*). Yet it is very hard to see how

Korzybski's objections to "a language of 'sensations' " apply to this sort of statement.

As we saw, it is very misleading to say that statements like "This water is warm" and (still worse) "This blade of grass is green" inevitably involve projecting some feeling or sensation onto the outside world and are therefore unreliable; but with such statements, and perhaps with any in which the "is" is followed by a common perceptual adjective, it is at least possible to understand the substance of Korzybski's objection. The qualities that such statements attribute to objects—sounds, smells, tastes, colors, "feels," and so on—are roughly what Locke called secondary qualities. His point was that such qualities (unlike others which he called primary or real) are "nothing in the objects themselves but powers to produce various sensations in us by their primary qualities, i.e. by the bulk, figure, texture, and motion of their insensible parts"*(Essay, II, viii, 10).* Since to describe how an object sounds or smells is to say how it sounds or smells to an observer under certain variable conditions, it has seemed natural to many thinkers to conclude that statements which attribute secondary qualities to objects are really statements about the "sensations" of the observer. Korzybski concluded further that the adjectives normally found in such statements refer to or name those sensations: "the events outside our skin are neither cold nor warm, green nor red, sweet nor bitter etc., but these characteristics are manufactured by our nervous system inside our skins, as responses only to different energy manifestations, physico-chemical processes, etc." *(p. 384).*

But what is the sensation or feeling we project onto the outside world when we make classificatory statements like "This is a dog"? Strange as it is to talk about "a feeling of 'green,' " it would be still stranger to talk about "a feeling of dog," or to say that just as nothing in the outside world is really red or green, so nothing is really a dog or a cat. The language of Korzybski's example suggests that what the man confused with something outside of him was his "verbal definition" of the term "dog"—that his mistake lay in thinking he was approaching his definition rather than something belonging to "the non-verbal, unspeakable objective level." Therefore this definition would seem to be the feeling Korzybski has in mind. Now of course we don't usually use the word "definition" to refer to a feeling or to anything remotely like a feeling, but rather to a verbal formulation of a word's meaning; and sometimes Korzybski uses the word in this ordinary way too. But here and at other points—when, for example, he tells us that the word "apple," "as it has no individual subscripts or date, is *not* a name for a definite object or stage of a process *which are all different,* but a name *for a definition"* (*p. 96*)—he seems rather to be thinking of definitions as one species of the "happenings in [our] nervous systems" (*LTA, p. 27*) that words stand for and that we designate as their meanings.

Now this is certainly an odd way to use the word "definition," but leaving that aside, it is still puzzling that Korzybski thinks the sort of inner happening named or referred to by common nouns like "dog" is a sensation or feeling rather than an idea or mental image. With similar statements, "Mr. Miller is a Jew" for example, Hayakawa says that the thing inside our heads we are confusing with Mr. Miller outside is not a sensation but rather a "high-level abstraction" (*LTA, p. 203*) or "notion" (*LTA, p. 204*). He makes it quite clear that a common noun like "dog" (or "cow," which is his example) refers to an "idea" or "concept," to "the characteristics we have abstracted as common to cow_1, cow_2, cow_3, ... cow_n" (*LTA, pp. 178–179*), and that the kind of noun that refers to an individual "object of perception" is not a common noun but a proper name—whether an ordinary one like "Bessie," a new one like "cow_1," or a demonstrative like "this," which general semanticists (and many twentieth-century philosophers) treat as a special sort of proper name. Given Korzybski's terminology, this seems the obvious conclusion: since he takes an "object of perception" to be a sensation or feeling, it would seem that in order to be consistent he would have to say that common nouns refer to ideas and proper names refer to sensations.[7]

But by this time it should be clear that consistency is not one of Korzybski's virtues, and though there are many other confusions in his treatment of subject-predicate statements, there is no use in examining them further. For reasons of his own (which, as we shall see, have nothing to do with language or its workings) he is determined to assert the unreliability of all subject-predicate statements; and since unreliability is closely associated in his mind with feelings, he simply concludes that all subject-predicate statements are really about feelings. In the case of the blade of grass, this involved assuming that there is a running correlation between our visual experience and processes accessible to the neurologist, even though such processes are in no sense the feelings or sensations Korzybski's theory demands. In the case of classificatory statements that end with a common noun, it involves going a step further and assuming a correlation between verbal behavior and even more

[7] Korzybski often does seem to hold this view—in fact I think his conception of the relation between ordinary language and mathematics, and therefore the whole drift of his argument as I paraphrased it above, depend on his holding it. That is why I attributed it to him (see p. 9, above) even though I could recall no place in which he had expressed it as clearly as Hayakawa does in the passage just quoted. It is only possible to criticize an argument that possesses a certain minimal degree of clarity; in setting about criticizing a writer like Korzybski it is sometimes necessary initially to provide more clarity than is actually there by deciding what intention must have lain behind the fog of words. It was also for this reason that I omitted mentioning in my paraphrase the whole notion of "a language of 'sensations,'" which seems to me to stand outside Korzybski's argument in a way I could not show at that point.

mysterious inner processes, such that whenever someone uses (or perhaps hears or thinks of) a word like
"dog," a particular idea or mental image or definition
is hauled up and placed before the eye of his mind.
It goes without saying that there is not a scrap of
scientific evidence for any such correlation.

Nor could there possibly be. The general mistake
about the origin and nature of language that lies
behind this mass of confusions and self-contradictions,
and behind Korzybski's recommendation about the
"is" of identity and his view that a language of
subject-predicate statements necessarily "deals with
entities *inside our skin*" *(p. 384),* is the idea that words
acquire meaning by being attached like labels to
inner experiences. As the sentence I quoted from
Locke on page 21 suggests, this idea has often been
advanced in conjunction with the conventionalist
myth. Not only for Locke but for Hobbes and Hume
as well, the origin of language is roughly the same
two-stage process as for Korzybski: first we all pri-
vately affix words to mental images or ideas which
have been obtained by abstraction from sense experience; then we all publicly agree to use the same word
as the "mark" or "sign" of similar ideas. Now one of
the triumphs of twentieth-century analytic philosophy
has been to show the dangers of thinking that there
is one relation that must hold between a meaningfully
used word and some extralinguistic entity that we designate as the word's meaning, and that this relation
is the one we often speak of indiscriminately as nam-
ing or referring to or symbolizing or standing for.[8] In

---

[8] Some good recent essays on this matter are Gilbert Ryle's
"The Theory of Meaning," in C. A. Mace (ed.), *British Philosophy in the Mid-Century* (London: Allen and Unwin, 1957), pp.
239–264; J. L. Austin's "The Meaning of a Word," reprinted in
his *Philosophical Papers* (Oxford: Oxford University Press, 1961),
pp. 23–43; Max Black's "Explanations of Meaning," reprinted in
his collection *Models and Metaphors* (Ithaca, N.Y.: Cornell
University Press, 1962), pp. 17–24; and W. P. Alston's "The
Quest for Meanings," *Mind,* LXXII (1963), 79–87. The historical

addition, Korzybski's (and Locke's) particular way of courting these dangers, by specifying that the entities in question are sensations or mental images (rather than physical objects, say), has its own special difficulties. The greatest of these is that such inner experiences cannot be produced for public inspection. How then can we ever be sure that someone else is using a word to refer to an idea similar to the one we use it to refer to? Of course he can describe or explain his idea, but only by using more words, each of which will raise the same question and so lead to an infinite regress.

It is important to understand that our inability to produce sensations or mental images for inspection is not due to a mere practical difficulty—as is, for example, the inability to produce bits of one's heart for inspection—but rather to a logical impossibility. For by definition nothing we would speak of as a sensation or a mental image could also be spoken of as ever being made accessible to anyone but the person having it—not even to a brain-surgeon or neurosurgeon, who may see a great deal else but does not see these things. Therefore, if it were true that words acquired their meaning by becoming attached to such inner experiences, it would be logically impossible not only to explain communication but even to know if communication ever took place, or even if there were a public world for it to take place about.[9] We saw that the conventionalist account of the origin of language is inadequate even if we assume that words stand for physical objects like books or

---

background of the position more or less shared by these essays is touched on by Professor Ryle and explained at length in two excellent little books, J. O. Urmson's *Philosophical Analysis* (Oxford: Oxford University Press, 1956) and G. J. Warnock's *English Philosophy Since 1900* (Oxford: Oxford University Press, 1958).

[9] Here I am indebted to Chapter II of Antony Flew, *Hume's Philosophy of Belief* (London: Routledge & Kegan Paul, 1961).

semanticists;[10] we can now see that its inadequacies are only compounded if we assume that "The meanings of words are . . . in US" *(LTA, p. 314)* rather than out in the world.

But there is an important difference between Korzybski and the earlier philosophers I mentioned above. Faced with the problem of showing how we ever get outside our private realms, the philosophers often just wave their theory of meaning aside and flatly assert not only the existence of a public world but also the possibilities of gaining real knowledge about it and of communicating that knowledge to others. Sometimes Korzybski takes an equally rough-and-ready way out by simply lumping ideas and mental images together with words as "higher order abstractions," and then telling us that such abstractions are "capable of being transmitted" *(p. 280)*, that they can be "recorded in books" *(p. 291)*, and that their "main importance" is "in their *public* character" *(p. 280)*. But while we often do speak of someone transmitting his ideas to others or recording them in books, when we do so we are speaking colloquially and are not using "idea" in the technical sense of "mental image." What we see on the page, after all, is the author's words, not his mental images.

But Korzybski has another, more elaborate route to the outside world: science. In what is perhaps his most concrete general specification of the way of talking we should adopt once we have dispensed with

[10] As Chase and Hayakawa sometimes do, when (probably under the influence of C. K. Ogden and I. A. Richards' *The Meaning of Meaning*) they lapse from Korzybski's "neurological attitude toward 'meaning'" (p. 22). These lapses occur more often in Chase, who follows Ogden and Richards in using the term "referent" to mean "the object or situation in the real world to which the word or label refers" *(TW, p. 9)* and accepts their view that "The point of every discussion is to *find the referent*" *(TW, p. 100)*. Chase even noticed and reported that "find the referent" was "a phrase which Korzybski did not like to use" *(PW, p. 147)*, but he does not seem to have understood why.

subject-predicate statements and the "is" of identity, he writes:

> If we use a language of adjectives and subject-predicate forms pertaining to "sense" impressions, we are using a language which deals with entities *inside our skin* and characteristics entirely non-existent in the outside world. Thus the events outside our skin are neither cold nor warm, green nor red, sweet nor bitter etc., but these characteristics are manufactured by our nervous system inside our skins, as responses only to different energy manifestations, physico-chemical processes, etc. When we use such terms, we are dealing with characteristics which are absent in the external world, and build up an anthropomorphic and delusional world non-similar in structure to the world around us. Not so if we use a language of order, relations, or structure, which can be applied to sub-microscopic events, to objective levels, to semantic levels, and which can also be expressed in words. *[p. 384]*

Unlike Locke, Korzybski here seems to be assuming that just ordinary words, not all words, refer to subjective inner experiences. If we do not use ordinary words for qualities and objects, but talk about them instead in "a language of order, relations, or structure" as "responses only to different energy manifestation, physico-chemical processes, etc.," then we will have escaped the narrow circuit of our own sensations and will be talking about external reality. But if this way out is more elaborate, it is no more satisfactory, for, as Black has shown, it only involves Korzybski in further contradictions and confusions:

> The characteristics ascribed to the scientific object, energy, electric and magnetic charge, and so on, are by no means experienced directly at what Korzybski calls the "unspeakable" level. They are, on the contrary, defined in terms of complicated manipulations of scientific instruments and calculated with the help of theoretical physics of a very high degree of abstractness. Now if we should assert, with Korzybski, that all abstractions are "manufactured by the nervous system" we should be compelled to say also that the "mad dance of electrons" constituting

the scientific object is likewise manufactured by the nervous system. . . . The reason for giving a superior status to the scientific object—for referring to it as a reality and to the series of abstractions emanating from it as shadows—was its alleged independence of what went on "inside our skins"; the swarm of electrons, unlike the abstractions derived from it, was *not* manufactured by the nervous system. If it be granted, however, that the scientific object, also, is a complex of abstract characteristics, the original basis for differentiation between reality and subjective abstractions disappears. *[Korzybski's "General Semantics," pp. 240–241]*

Furthermore, from a practical standpoint it is so obviously impossible for us all to go around all of the time talking about ultimate particles and energy manifestations, rather than about brown tables and red apples, that not even Korzybski can quite bring himself to suggest we try it. In fact, the extreme vagueness of the specific alternatives he does suggest makes it clear that by "a language of order, relations, or structure" he merely means a language possessing these terms, and that by speaking such a language he merely means using the terms now and then—he doesn't much care how we use them or what particular assertions we make with them. So his persistent faith in the wonders that will *"automatically"* be wrought by "the habitual use of a *few new terms" (p. 63)* is really nothing more nor less than a singularly pure example of that primitive "belief in word-magic" he and his followers are so fond of finding everywhere but in their own work and that of recent scientists and social scientists. This belief Hayakawa aptly defines as "the notion that, by *saying* things repeatedly or in specified ceremonial ways, we can cast a spell over the future and force events to turn out the way we said they would" *(LTA, pp. 109–110).*

Most of the time, however, general semanticists do not even offer us an alternative, and most of the time, as in Korzybski's example about the dog, the real difficulty does not seem to have anything to do with language. Certainly something went wrong in that example, but why blame it on the word "dog" or on the statement "This is a dog"? Since we do not always respond verbally to objects entering our field of vision, and since (other things being equal) the man presumably would have got bitten no matter what he had said or even if he had said nothing, it might be better to say that his mistake lay in deciding or inferring it was a dog rather than in *saying* any particular thing. But this seems wrong too since after all it *was* a dog, even if it did bite. What does Korzybski want us to call it, if not a dog?

I think Korzybski himself senses the difficulty, not only because he fails to offer any alternative term or statement but also because he suggests that the real cause of the trouble was not the words the man used but rather his "associations" with the term "dog" and the "expectations" it raised in him. This seems right enough, but then it looks like what Korzybski is trying to bring about is not a change in the structure of our language as a whole but merely a change in our "associations" and "expectations," in the degree of knowledge or awareness with which we use certain words or expressions. This is not surprising when we recall that the end to be achieved by revising our language was in fact a new state of awareness, "consciousness of abstracting." But Korzybski's theory of meaning, by asserting that words either stand for or actually are ideas or sensations, leads him to confuse language with knowledge and to assume that the man who got bitten was asserting (with inevitable falsity) the completeness of his knowledge about dogs merely because he used the word "dog" in a subject-predicate statement. The relation between these two very different sorts of change never emerges clearly in Korzybski, nor does it in Chase and Hayakawa, who sidestep the issue by putting almost all of their emphasis on achieving consciousness of abstracting and merely pay lip service to the idea that we should revise the structure of our language. As with the idea that language was instituted by agreement, this difference between Korzybski and his popularizers is probably due to the fact that they are more interested in practice and less in theory than he is: for while changing people's attitudes or associations is certainly not always easy, it is less absurdly ambitious than trying to change the structure of English.

Hayakawa, as we have seen, makes a certain sense of the index numbers by reducing them to mere mnemonic devices—though of course saying to ourselves "Cow$_1$ is not cow$_2$" accomplishes nothing that is not accomplished more naturally by saying "Bessie and Daisy are (two different) cows" *(see LTA, p. 178)*. In the same way he reduces and internalizes Korzybski's other major recommendation to a warning that we "Beware of the word 'is,' which, when not used simply as an auxiliary verb ('he is coming'), can"—but by implication need not—"crystallize misevaluations" *(LTA, p. 315)*. To see the difference we need only put this against Korzybski's firm insistence that we "must abandon permanently the use of the 'is' of identity" *(p. 60)* because it "always introduces false evaluation" *(p. 374)*. Hayakawa's objection to the statement "Mr. Miller is a Jew" is merely that

"Jew" is only *one* of thousands upon thousands of abstractions which may be applied to Mr. Miller, to whom such terms as "left-hander," "parent," "amateur golfer," "history teacher," "teetotaler," "Bostonian," and so on may possibly be equally applied. But the prejudiced person is unaware of all but the one abstraction—perhaps in most contexts the least relevant one— "Jew." *[LTA, p. 203]*

Presumably after we are aware of what else Mr. Miller is, there is nothing wrong with saying "Mr. Miller is a Jew." But if that's true, then there never was anything wrong with the statement itself—any more than with "This is a dog"—but only with the ways in which our "associations" with the term "Jew" might have encouraged us to act on the statement.

What we can see in Hayakawa's treatment of the two recommendations we can see elsewhere as well: Korzybski's popularizers manage to make sense of his idea of linguistic revision only by translating it into terms that have nothing to do with language but only with knowledge or awareness. High-level abstractions are the most suspect and dangerous sort of linguistic expression for the general semanticist, yet Hayakawa sensibly tells us there is nothing wrong with using them provided we know what we are talking about:

The test of abstractions then is not whether they are "high-" or "low-level" abstractions, but *whether they are referrable to lower levels.* If one makes a statement about "culinary arts in America," one should be able to refer the statement down the abstraction ladder to particulars of American restaurants, American domestic science, American techniques of food preservation, down to Mrs. Levin in her kitchen. [*LTA, pp. 187–188*]

Similarly, Chase writes:

Adam$_1$ says: "I don't like Harvard University. I wouldn't send my boy there." The statement is meaningless as it stands. What is it that you do not like, Mr. Adam? . . . *What things? In what place? When?*

If Adam$_1$ made a list of those characteristics of Harvard in 1938 which he did like and another of those which he did not like, and found the second more impressive, he might properly say that so far as he knew the circumstances, there were more characteristics of which he disapproved than there were that he approved. Or he might say that a single negative factor outweighed in his mind a large number of positive factors. He could shorten this to "I don't like Harvard," provided he were fully conscious of the abstraction, or short cut, taken. [*TW, p. 92*]

But how can the statement "I don't like Harvard (University)" be "meaningless as it stands" and yet become meaningful if the person who makes it has good reasons for doing so? If the statement were genuinely meaningless, how could you ever gather good reasons for it or know what questions to ask another person to find out whether or not he had such reasons? Since the statement itself undergoes no change, it would be more accurate to say that it is vague or unclear as it stands.

The fact is that Korzybski's theories about language and the structure of language make no sense when taken literally, and his grand design of linguistic revision boils down in practice to the helpful (if obvious) rule of thumb that we should always know what we are talking about and be prepared to back up our statements with appropriate and convincing examples. But of course we don't need science to tell us what common sense told us long ago. Whatever pretensions general semantics has to being a science of meaning depend rather on the truth or falsity of the description it offers of the nature of language and of the relations between language and the world. Since the description is extremely confused and at points even self-contradictory, the pretensions are (to say the least) unfulfilled.

III

But it is not enough merely to show that Korzybski's theories about language are untenable and that his attempt to create a science of meaning is therefore a failure, for after all his stress was, as Hayakawa reminds us, "on education and mental hygiene" (SSP, p. 113), on the beneficial ethical and social results that would be achieved by applying his theories. To his credit, Korzybski would never have defended theories he recognized as untenable merely on the ground that they seemed to produce desirable results, but I have heard general semanticists argue in this way and so it seems worthwhile also to examine the suitability of the theories to the aims Korzybski thought they would accomplish. I shall try to show that in addition to being untenable in themselves, Korzybski's theories inhibit and even discourage the accomplishment of his social aims.

We have seen that Korzybski's recommendations about changing the structure of language make sense only when they are translated into recommendations about changing people's knowledge or awareness, and that his confused theory of meaning helps to blur the distinction between these two very different enterprises. What we must now ask is whether the specific change in awareness he wants to bring about, the change that would result in universal "consciousness of abstracting," would in turn bring about the further change in people's behavior demanded for the accomplishment of his social aims. Now from the sort of subject-predicate statements he and his followers most often choose as examples—"This boy is lazy," "Joe is a radical," "She is bad," "Mr. Miller is a Jew," and so on—it is clear that the change in behavior they want to bring about is a change in the direction of tolerance and open-mindedness. I think the real reason Korzybski mounts his attack on subject-predicate statements—the reason I referred to earlier on p. 33 as having nothing to do with language—is that narrow-minded people often fix obsessively on one character trait or one fact about another person's history and refuse to take anything else into account. This fact led Korzybski to suspect that there must be something wrong with the kind of statement we usually use to categorize people or objects and to attribute qualities to them. He concluded that what he calls subject-predicate statements always have, by virtue of their form alone and regardless of content or context, the blind finality they have when a bigot uses them to voice a prejudice. Therefore he insisted that "x is (a) y" really means "x is a y and nothing else" or "x is completely *y*" or (most generally) "*x* is identical with *y*-ness." We have seen the absurdity of the theories he constructed to justify this conclusion, and now that we see the motives behind them, we must not let our sympathy with those motives lead us to forget the absurdity of the theories. When people categorize rigidly, they often do seem to be attributing a mysterious potency to words or slogans, but this fact does not allow us to place so much of the blame for human frailty on language. Whatever makes a bigot a bigot, it isn't language. The fact that we often react rigidly or mechanically to the world has no more to do with the structure of English (or any other language) than not knowing dogs sometimes bite had to do with the form of the statement "This is a dog."

But what if we grant this and then go on to ask whether consciousness of abstracting—a simultaneous awareness of similarities and differences in our experience—would, however achieved, necessarily produce the desired tolerance? Look again at Hayakawa's treatment of the statement "Mr. Miller is a Jew." We have seen that after we are aware of what else Mr. Miller is, of all the respects in which he is similar to and different from other people, there is nothing wrong with the statement itself. Now suppose we tried Hayakawa's arguments on a "prejudiced person," pointing out to him all the other abstractions that could be applied to Mr. Miller, and he patiently replied as follows: "Of course I know all that: if I were getting up a baseball team I might be interested in his being a left-hander, and if I were organizing a chapter of the Parent-Teacher Association I might be interested in his being a parent; but as it happens, I am interested in keeping Jews out of the neighborhood because they lower property values, and so I am only interested in the fact that he's a Jew." If he knew his general semantics, he might even cite Hayakawa to the effect that "What we call things and where we draw the line between one class of things and another depend upon the interests we have and the purposes of the classification" because classification "is simply a reflection of social convenience and necessity" *(LTA, pp. 215, 217)*. Or he might refer to Chase's remark that if "a single negative factor outweighed . . . a large number of positive factors" *(TW, p. 92)* in the mind of the man who didn't like Harvard, then there was nothing wrong with his saying (and presumably acting on) "I don't like Harvard." By analogy, what can possibly be wrong with saying (and acting on) "I don't like Jews" if you have carefully decided that for reasons of "social convenience and necessity" the one "negative factor" outweighs all the others?

Now to reply as Hayakawa suggests, that " 'Jew' is perhaps one of the most sloppily constructed abstractions in the language—that is, one of the most difficult to refer systematically . . . to lower levels" *(LTA, p. 203)*, is obviously no answer at all. For if classificatory systems are arbitrary and words have no meaning in themselves, our anti-Semite could very easily cooperate with like-minded neighbors in setting up a precise and workable definition, just as the Nazis did in the thirties. Nor would it do to fall back on talking about "survival value." Imagine yourself having a drink on a spacious terrace somewhere in suburban Connecticut and trying to convince your host, a well-heeled New York corporation executive, that by belonging to a restricted country club he was appreciably damaging his chances of survival! Or imagine yourself arguing for Negro voting rights with a rural Southern politician who knew perfectly well that at least his political (if not his physical) survival depended precisely on his keeping the racist sentiments of his constituents stirred up. It seems not only that there is nothing wrong with the statement "Mr. Miller is a Jew," but that there is not even anything wrong with the bigoted attitudes and actions that sometimes accompany such statements.

What are we to do? The answer we want to give,

and the answer Chase and Hayakawa would give if their theories allowed them to, is of course that a prejudiced person is an unconditionally bad thing to be—not because being one will involve you in using sloppily constructed abstractions or will decrease your chances of survival, but simply because your actions will probably be unjust and may have bad effects on the lives of other people. Chase does at one point observe that "Korzybski, in his semantic analysis, often indicates a standard of judgment which we have long associated with toleration toward our fellow creatures and kindness in our treatment of them," but he feels compelled to add immediately (with a show of tough-mindedness and "science") that Korzybski "adopts this standard not because he is inspired with 'love for humanity,' but because it is the conclusion which the facts seem to warrant" *(TW, pp. 78–79)*. Leaving aside the question of whether or not it would be such a bad thing simply to be "inspired with 'love for humanity,' " one wants to ask just what facts Chase has in mind—the fact that nothing is identical with anything else? As we have seen, if all classificatory systems are strictly neutral and can be justified purely by their usefulness, it need not concern an anti-Semite that "Jew_1 is not Jew_2," any more than it need concern those of us not interested in birdwatching that "Evening $grosbeak_1$ is not evening $grosbeak_2$," for the simple fact of an object's uniqueness tells us absolutely nothing about how we ought to behave towards the object. An intelligent anti-Semite would undoubtedly be well aware that by saying "Mr. Miller is a Jew" he was not denying that every Jew is different from every other (and indeed from everything else in the universe) any more than he was confusing Mr. Miller with a word or sensation or mental image. And once he had demonstrated his recognition of this, and had explained that he was merely saying that the one respect in which Mr. Miller was like other Jews was enough to make him objectionable, it is difficult to imagine what more Korzybski's theories would entitle Hayakawa to say in reply. This would seem a serious drawback if one's aim is to promote tolerance and open-mindedness; just how serious it is will become clear if we see how Hayakawa deals with an actual social issue—perhaps the most important one of our time.

In an essay called "The Fully Functioning Personality" he quotes approvingly from the psychologist A. H. Maslow:

> One does not complain about water because it is wet, nor about rocks because they are hard. . . . As the child looks out upon the world with wide, uncritical and innocent eyes, simply noting and observing what is the case, without either arguing the matter or demanding that it be otherwise, so does the self-actualizing person look upon human nature both in himself and others. [Quoted SSP, p. 64]

And in another essay, "The Self-Image and Intercultural Understanding, Or How To Be Sane Though Negro," Hayakawa recommends this attitude to Negroes. After recounting all the areas "at the level of facts" in which "it can be said that the fight for desegregation, and therefore equality, has already been won" (SSP, p. 74), he concludes that "progress is inevitable" and that "Negroes simply cannot lose" (SSP, p. 87). If this seems difficult to realize, that is only because

> . . . at the level of words, white Southerners are writing the same kind of speeches they have uttered for the past twenty years . . . [and] the National Association for the Advancement of Colored People and the Negro newspapers and the Negro spokesmen . . . continue to give the same angry speeches and write the same fiery editorials that they have for the past twenty years. [SSP, p. 79]

In Hayakawa's view, Negroes should learn instead "to forget as far as possible that [they are] Negro" (SSP, p. 77), to "[take] equality for granted" (SSP, p. 80), and to "act as the white man's psychotherapist" *(SSP, p. 82):*

> Why get angry with these poor, ignorant, sick people who are trying to be friendly? Why not give them a C-minus for effort and forget it? . . . If you expect too much of them—if you expect all white people to be intelligent and sensible on the subject of Negroes—you will be running into daily disappointments. If, however, your expectations are realistic—in other words, if you expect four out of five white persons to be pretty ignorant on the subject—then you will be delighted when the score for a given day turns out to be only three out of five. *[SSP, pp. 80–81]*

This advice evidently follows from Korzybski's principle that "minimum expectation" is "the basis of happiness,"[11] which Hayakawa illustrates by the following anecdote:

> Years ago I used to notice the differences among motormen on the Indiana Avenue streetcar line in Chicago—a street often blocked by badly parked cars and huge trailer trucks backing into warehouses and maneuvering in everybody's way. Some motormen seemed to expect to be able to drive down Indiana Avenue without interruption. Every time they got blocked, they would get steamed up with rage, clang their bells and lean out of their cars to shout at the truck drivers. At the end of a day these motormen must have been nervous wrecks; I can imagine them coming home at the end of a day, jittery and hypersensitive, a menace to their wives and children. Other motormen, however, seemed to expect Indiana Avenue to be heavily blocked —a realistic expectation, because it usually was. They could sit and wait for minutes without impatience, calmly whistling a tune, cleaning their fingernails, or writing their reports. In other words, confronting the same objective situation, some motormen lived a hellish life of anger and nervous tension; other motor-

---

[11] Cf. "In life, numerous serious 'hurts' occur precisely because we do not appreciate some natural shortcomings and expect *too much*. Expecting too much leads to very harmful semantic shocks, disappointments, suspicions, fears, hopelessness, helplessness, pessimism, etc." (p. 472).

men had a nice, relaxing job, with plenty of time for rest. *[SSP, p. 81]*

I had better admit at once that I find this offensive. Why should Negroes have to forget they are Negroes? And why should Negroes unwilling merely to look "out upon the world with wide, uncritical and innocent eyes" and to keep their expectations minimal be compared to Hayakawa's admittedly irrational motormen? Isn't there a difference between expecting to be treated decently and expecting "to be able to drive down Indiana Avenue without interruption"? And on top of settling for so little, why should Negroes be forced to take on the additional burden of being "the white man's psychotherapist"? I would not blame a Negro for regarding this as an invitation to a new and more subtle kind of servitude. Of course nothing could be further from Hayakawa's intent, but it is both puzzling and disturbing that this offensive advice should come from a man who otherwise sounds so candid and decent.

More important, Hayakawa's argument would probably seem puzzling even to a racist who did not find it either disturbing or offensive. What would puzzle him, I think, is that Hayakawa is clearly in favor of the gains Negroes have made in achieving social and political equality, yet he classes the militant speeches that were instrumental in achieving those gains together with the speeches of white Southerners intent on preventing their achievement and recommends that Negroes stop being militant and adopt an attitude of uncritical passivity. The Negro leaders who for twenty years have had "their attention fixed on how much farther there [was] to go rather than on how far we have come" seem to him just as unrealistic as the white Southerners who have been defending "the unalterable traditions of the South" *(SSP, p. 79)*, and just as irrelevant to whatever progress Negroes have made and will continue to make in the future. "Times are changing" at the level of facts, he tells us, while "At the level of words, . . . thing [sic] *sound* pretty much the same as they did twenty years ago" *(SSP, pp. 78–79)*. The implication is that nobody's words had anything to do with changing the facts of the Negro's situation. Moreover, the analogy of the motormen seems to suggest that even the actions performed in response to some of those words—concerted, purposeful social and political actions like the staging of demonstrations and the writing of letters to congressmen—had little or nothing to do with changing things.

Yet Hayakawa freely admits that "Twenty years ago, . . . People really lived in a more severely segregated world than we now do in urban centers throughout the United States" *(SSP, p. 74)*, so he must think something happened to cause the change—but what was it? How did the fight ever get won? How and when did progress become inevitable? Perhaps the one thing the Governor of Alabama and the head of the NAACP would agree on is what Hayakawa implicitly denies: that the words of people who had "their attention fixed on how much farther there [was] to go rather than how far we have come," together with the actions that accompanied and dramatized those words, had a great deal to do with winning the fight. For whether or not one thinks the changes Hayakawa is talking about add up to progress, it seems very odd to call them inevitable. Indeed a racist might well say that things could have been quite different, and the status quo maintained, if only Negroes had continued to expect little and to look "out upon the world with wide, uncritical and innocent eyes, simply noting and observing what is the case, without either arguing the matter or demanding that it be otherwise." Maslow's "self-actualizing person," invested with a black skin, looks very much like the traditional image of the "good darky."

For Hayakawa, however, the changes that have

taken place in civil rights are the result of vast implacable forces operating as physical laws operate, without the intervention of conscious human agency: "The moral sense of the nation (except in a few pockets of resistance)," he tells us, "economic conditions, technological necessities, historical social forces both here and abroad, and, most importantly, the practical necessities of living together in our extremely close-knit and interdependent economy will compel" —and presumably these are what have so far compelled—"the end of enforced segregation, both official and unofficial" *(SSP, p. 87)*. The whole business has a curiously passive and impersonal air. The actions Hayakawa takes as indications that the fight is won and progress inevitable are not purposeful actions performed in response to anybody's words but are "wordless" and almost involuntary:

> At the level of facts . . . hundreds of thousands of ordinary people, white and Negro, who twenty years ago used to lunch separately, are now eating together in factory lunchrooms, school cafeterias, hamburger stands, dining cars, and other places of public refreshment. But the trouble with an uneventful lunch at which whites and Negroes manage to get down their blue-plate specials without having a riot, is that it can never get into the papers. It is, in a curious way, a wordless experience—people simply eat their lunches and pay their checks, and the national offices of neither the NAACP nor the Ku Klux Klan get any word of it. *[SSP, p. 79]*

Now one cause of the strangeness of Hayakawa's argument is obviously his determination to maintain Korzybski's strict separation between verbal and non-verbal levels, between "the level of words" and "the level of facts": the fact that nobody's words about an event *are* the event (which nobody would quarrel with) leads Hayakawa to imply that nobody's words *had any influence on* the particular events he is talking about—and that, as we have seen, is a quite different conclusion .which almost everybody would want to quarrel with. Moreover, in the neutrality with which he regards the speeches of the Negro leaders and the white Southerners—a neutrality that is hard to reconcile with his views on civil rights and therefore seems oddly studied and artificial—I think we can see the influence of the analogy Korzybski used to express the relation between verbal and nonverbal levels once he had asserted their separation, the analogy between languages and maps.

The most obvious reason the analogy appealed to Korzybski is that he took map-making as a sort of paradigm of scientific activity, and therefore of sane behavior. For him science was the accurate observation and recording of data, the making of predictions on the basis of these data, and the careful checking and rechecking of the predictions against new data; and this is of course how maps actually do get made. Once a territory has initially been mapped, the cartographer's job is to keep his map up to date by observing and recording topographical changes, without in any way trying to cause or prevent them. Therefore, one implication of the analogy is that the function (or at least the main function) of language is to provide a realistic description of change. This is what Hayakawa accuses both groups of speakers of having failed to do and what he himself is endeavoring to do by preserving a neutrality towards them something like the objectivity with which it is proper for the cartographer to regard his territory. Now we can certainly agree that neither the Negro spokesmen nor the white Southerners have been content simply to describe the changes taking place in civil rights, and so if the analogy were an apt one, Hayakawa's objection would be well taken and his neutrality appropriate; but the strangeness of his argument suggests that his objection is not well taken and that his neutrality is inappropriate, and therefore that the analogy may not be apt. To find out whether it is or not, let's return to Korzybski for just a moment.

One of the most important and surprising points in

the argument of *Science and Sanity,* as I paraphrased it above, is the point at which the map analogy enters, the point at which Korzybski concludes that because "words *are not* the objects which they represent, *structure, and structure alone,* becomes the only link which connects our verbal processes with the empirical data" *(p. 59),* and that therefore since "A map *is not* the territory it represents, but, if correct, it has a *similar structure* to the territory," languages "must be considered *only as maps*" *(p. 58).* Again we are quite ready to agree that words are not identical with the objects or events we use them to talk about—indeed it is hard to understand just what it would mean to disagree and equally hard to imagine that anyone has ever done so. But why should Korzybski go on to conclude from this that languages are in some fundamental way like maps? We might be less surprised if his main point had been that just as most words "have no meaning in themselves" but "are as purely symbolic as *x, y,* and *z*" *(TW, p. 54),* so in making a map we can arbitrarily decide to use either crosses or dots for cities, dotted or continuous lines for rivers, and so on. For the conventionality of a map's symbols (or "vocabulary") really does make it something like a language. But of course the thing that interests him about maps is that an accurate one must reflect or reproduce the spatial arrangement of its territory. Now ordinarily when we speak of the structure of a language, we mean its grammar and sound system, and of course it is impossible to think of these as in any way reflecting or reproducing the structure of the outside world or the nervous system or anything else. But from what we have seen of Korzybski's recommendations for changing the structure of English, we know that his notion of linguistic structure is quite different from this ordinary one.

As my paraphrase suggested, Korzybski arrives at his notion of linguistic structure by (implicitly) extending to whole languages his view that sentences have meaning by virtue of fitting or corresponding to actual or possible states of affairs—i.e., by virtue of reproducing their structures as a map reproduces the structure of its territory. This theory of sentence-meaning has been held by a good many philosophers and is capable of considerable elaboration, even though it is ultimately unsatisfactory.[12] What gives it its initial plausibility is probably that an ordinary sentence, like a map or picture, can be seen all at once and its structure can therefore be taken in at a glance. Also, the sort of simple declarative sentence usually considered by the theory's adherents *states* that something is the case, and this can seem very much like what a map does when it *shows* Boston a certain distance from New York, say, or Texas bigger than Indiana. But in the case of whole languages the theory does not have even this initial plausibility, for we cannot see the whole of English or any other language all at once (whatever that would mean) and, more important, it seems absurd to think of a whole language as stating or asserting something in particular.

Yet of course this is exactly what Korzybski is doing when he tells us that just as a meaningful sentence reflects in its structure that of some state of affairs, so "every language . . . reflects in its own structure that of the world as assumed by those who evolved the language" *(pp. 59–60),* that therefore "a language, any language, has at its bottom certain metaphysics" *(p. 89),* and even that language "enslaves us" because "the structure which a language exhibits, and impresses upon us unconsciously, is *automatically projected* upon the world around us" *(p. 90).* Thus it is on the notion that each language necessarily embodies a particular world-view that Korzybski's analogy of languages and

[12] For a detailed and persuasive demonstration of its shortcomings, see E. Daitz, "The Picture Theory of Meaning," in Antony Flew (ed.), *Essays in Conceptual Analysis* (London: Macmillan, 1956), pp. 53–74. Urmson's *Philosophical Analysis* is again extremely helpful on the historical background.

maps depends, but from what we have seen of his efforts to prove English "a language of 'sensations,'" we should now be able to see that this notion is sheer fantasy. A world-view or "metaphysics" is a body of interrelated assertions, but since all natural languages contain devices for negation, anything that can be asserted in a given language can just as easily—from a linguistic, as opposed to a cultural, point of view—be denied in it. Of course we can sometimes predict accurately what the speakers of a given language will say (or write or think) about the cause of storms, say, or how to insure a good harvest; but to make such predictions we need to know a good deal about their culture, not just their language alone. An infinite number of sentences can be formed in accordance with the rules of any given language, and if all we know about the speakers of a language is the rules of their language, we can make no predictions whatever about which of these sentences they will actually speak or write (let alone think), for a language is one thing and the verbal (let alone mental) behavior of its speakers is something quite different.

In the example about the dog, we saw that Korzybski confused knowing (how to use) a particular word with having some particular definition of it in mind or particular knowledge about what it referred to, and using the word with asserting the adequacy of one's definition or the completeness of one's knowledge. His comparison of languages to maps, and his and other people's abortive efforts to extract a "metaphysics" from a particular language, whether English or Hopi[13] or Chinese, make the same mistake on a grander scale by confusing knowing (how to speak) a particular

[13] In mentioning Hopi I am of course thinking of the writings of Benjamin Lee Whorf, now conveniently collected in *Language, Thought and Reality* (Cambridge, Mass.: M.I.T. Press, 1956). The definitive refutation of Whorf is Max Black's "Linguistic Relativity: The Views of Benjamin Lee Whorf," in *Models and Metaphors*, pp. 244–257.

language with having a particular view of the world and speaking the language with asserting the truth of the view.

Like his two recommendations, then, Korzybski's analogy is the result of his having confused language with attitudes or knowledge; and just as when they try to follow his recommendations, so when they try to apply the analogy, his disciples translate it into a statement about knowledge rather than about language. Hayakawa, for example, introduces the analogy by telling us that "Most of our knowledge, acquired from parents, friends, schools, newspapers, books, conversation, speeches, and television, is received *verbally*" *(LTA, p. 30),* and it is this knowledge, not the structure of English, that he tells us must function as a map of the outside world.

But translation can no more salvage the analogy than it could the recommendations. Why should the main goal of thinking (and presumably of speaking) be to map or describe the world as it changes? Often, particularly in the case of social or political changes, we also try to judge and perhaps to influence what is happening. Certainly that is what the white Southerners and the Negro spokesmen Hayakawa reproaches for being unrealistic were trying to do. They had no intention of merely describing the changes taking place in civil rights, but rather were recommending (and attempting to justify) certain courses of action which would either halt or speed up those changes. Since this is often a natural (and necessary) thing to do, our appraisal of the two sorts of speakers should not depend on whether they offer us a realistic description but on whether the courses of action they recommend are morally admirable and whether their arguments are sound. After all, the fact that a change is occurring at a certain rate does not mean that it ought to occur at that rate or even that it ought to occur at all. Perhaps some things (like equality for Negroes) ought to come faster than they are coming, or perhaps some things (like the traditions of the South) are worth preserving and ought not to be changed.

As Hayakawa's inability (or unwillingness) to make any distinction between the white Southerners and the Negro spokesmen makes clear, his theories give him no way of arguing questions like these, just as they gave him no way of arguing with the anti-Semite that certain "factors" ought not to "outweigh" certain others in the decisions we make about our conduct. And just as Hayakawa would have nothing further to say once the anti-Semite had demonstrated his awareness that each Jew was bound to differ from everybody else in some way or other, so he would have nothing further to say to either the white Southerners or the Negro spokesmen once they had shown their awareness of the changes actually taking place in civil rights. And this would hardly be difficult for them to do; far from being uninformed about these changes, they are probably better informed about them than anyone else in the country.

So despite Korzybski's intense interest in promoting social change, when his theories are applied to actual social problems they tend to encourage conformity or even inaction, the self-embalmed accepting passivity suggested by Maslow's definition of the self-actualizing person. We can see, then, that general semantics fails on two counts: first, it does not yield the clearer view of the world that its practitioners promise; second, that clearer view, no matter how it was attained, would not necessarily lead us to tolerate and cooperate with each other any better than we do now. Later, when we are in a better position to understand some of the further implications of Korzybski's failure to construct a science of meaning, we shall return to it. We must now ask what his failure, and some of the mistakes about language that we have seen to lie behind it, can teach us to expect from a genuinely scientific treatment of meaning.

linguistics
and
meaning

It should be clear by now that we could not expect a science of meaning to give us a mechanical way of telling valid from invalid arguments or appropriate from inappropriate examples—let alone to make us more tolerant. But to say this is to say the obvious; to go further, recall the two most important mistaken assumptions about language that emerged from our examination of general semantics. Put in their most general form these two assumptions are: (1) that the meaning of a word or expression is best thought of as some sort of extralinguistic entity, and that the word or expression is meaningful (or "has meaning") by virtue of standing for or symbolizing or referring to or being in some other way conventionally correlated with this entity; (2) that the structure of a particular natural language either actually or ideally corresponds to or reflects or pictures the structure of the world. Therefore in our attempt to discover what we could expect from a genuinely scientific treatment of meaning we might begin by saying that we could expect it to provide more adequate characterizations of these two notions, the *meaning* of a word or expression and the *structure* of a language.

Earlier I mentioned in passing the success with which recent philosophers have criticized the first of these two mistaken assumptions. I was thinking of the philosophers usually—though, as we shall see, somewhat misleadingly—referred to as "ordinary language" philosophers. The main influence upon their work has been the later work of Wittgenstein, and the criticisms I had in mind had their beginnings in his famous enigmatic injunction: "Don't ask for the meaning, ask for the use." In his essay "The Theory of Meaning" Gilbert Ryle takes this injunction to mean that "the meaning of an expression is not an entity denoted by it, but a style of operation performed with it, not a nominee but a rôle,"[1] and he comments further:

> . . . the notion of meaning came now to be seen as somehow compact of rules. To know what an expression means involves knowing what can (logically) be said with it and what cannot (logically) be said with it. It involves knowing a set of bans, fiats and obligations, or, in a word, it is to know the rules of the employment of that expression. . . . Learning the meaning of an expression is more like learning a piece of drill than like coming across a previously unencountered object. It is learning to operate correctly with an expression and with any other expression equivalent to it. *[pp. 254, 256–257]*

I think it is fair to say generally that whenever ordinary language philosophers have faced the question

[1] C. A. Mace (ed.), *British Philosophy in the Mid-Century* (London: Allen and Unwin, 1957), p. 262.

SEMANTICS, LINGUISTICS, AND CRITICISM

directly, they have recommended that we think of the meaning of a word as the word's logical or conceptual role as determined by the rules of the language.

But so far as I know, these philosophers have not offered any general characterization of linguistic structure to compete with or supplant Korzybski's. They are mainly interested in examining the logic of particular linguistic expressions to get at the nature of certain traditional philosophical problems, and while this interest has sometimes led them to advance important claims about the general nature of language,[2] they have (in the words of one recent critic) "done almost nothing in the way of theorizing about linguistic structure," and their "concern with linguistic details . . . [has gone] hand in hand with a failure to take into account the complex structural organization in which such facts are systematized in actual languages."[3] As one ordinary language philosopher has written:

. . . we do not in philosophy need to state precisely what are the necessary and sufficient conditions for calling a signalling system a language; for we are not particularly concerned with defining the word "language." Nor are we concerned with a systematic classification of the different grammatical forms of language; the interest of contemporary philosophers in forms of speech neither is, nor should be, scientific or systematic.[4]

Since this sort of scientific or systematic interest is precisely what is needed to develop an adequate conception of linguistic structure, and since it is

[2] One example is Wittgenstein's claim about the impossibility of "private languages." Several of the most important essays on this problem are collected in George Pitcher (ed.), *Wittgenstein: The "Philosophical Investigations"* (Garden City, N.Y.: Anchor Books, 1966).

[3] Jerrold J. Katz, *The Philosophy of Language* (New York: Harper & Row, 1966), p. 88.

[4] Stuart Hampshire, "The Interpretation of Language: Words and Concepts," in *British Philosophy in the Mid-Century* (New York: Humanities Press), 2nd ed., p. 267.

linguists—and particularly American linguists—rather than philosophers who have taken such an interest, it is to linguistics that we must turn now, though we shall return to ordinary language philosophy later.

I

As any reader of this book will probably be well aware, the sort of linguistics practiced and taught by American linguists has made enormous advances in the last thirty or forty years. From an obscure discipline known only to a few specialists, it has come to be widely regarded as (in Stuart Chase's words) "the most exact of all the social sciences,"[5] to be taught at most of our universities, and to exert a powerful influence on American education. The theoretical foundation for these advances is usually said to have been laid by the Swiss linguist Ferdinand de Saussure. In his posthumously published *Cours de linguistique générale*[6] de Saussure drew a sharp distinction between synchronic or static linguistics, which studies languages individually and independently as systematic wholes, and diachronic or evolutionary linguistics, which studies "not relations between co-existing terms of a language-state but relations between successive terms that are substituted for each other in time" *(p. 140)*. He asserted that the two kinds of linguistics "are not of equal importance" but that "the synchronic view predominates" *(p. 90)*. Since nineteenth-century linguistics had (in de Saussure's

[5] *The Power of Words* (New York: Harcourt Brace Jovanovich, 1954), p. 100.

[6] Though this important work appeared in 1916, it has only recently been made available in an English translation by Wade Baskin, as *Course in General Linguistics* (New York: Philosophical Library, 1959). All subsequent page references to de Saussure are to this version.

words) been "completely absorbed in diachrony" *(p. 82)*, having occupied itself specifically with the study of sound changes, what he was recommending for linguistics was nothing less than a reversal of direction. That American linguists view their discipline as having come into being as a result of this reversal of direction is attested by the fact that they often refer to it as "descriptive" or "structural" linguistics precisely in order to distinguish it from nineteenth-century historical or comparative linguistics. In his book *Language*, usually regarded as the definitive text in American linguistics, Leonard Bloomfield credits de Saussure with having been one of the first linguists to insist "upon descriptive study as a basis for both historical research and philosophical generalization."[7] And Bloomfield, like de Saussure, objects to the nineteenth-century idea that "the only aspect of language worth studying is its change in the course of time" *(p. 18)*.

There are important differences between Bloomfield's and de Saussure's conceptions of their subject, however, and we must understand these as well if we are to understand the notion of linguistic structure which American linguists have developed. One place these differences emerge is in the contrast between the ways the two men view the history of linguistics. After the sentence I quoted above in which he condemns his immediate predecessors for having been "completely absorbed in diachrony," de Saussure writes:

> **Against this, what was the procedure of those who studied language before the beginning of modern [i.e., nineteenth-century] linguistics, i.e. the "grammarians" inspired by traditional methods? It is curious to note that here their viewpoint was absolutely above reproach. Their works clearly show that they tried to describe language-states. Their program was strictly synchronic . . .**

[7] (New York: Holt, Rinehart & Winston, 1933), p. 19.

> Classical grammar has been criticized as unscientific; still, its basis is less open to criticism and its data are better defined than is true of the [diachronic] linguistics started by Bopp. *[p. 82]*

Thus for de Saussure the reversal of direction involved in the shift from a diachronic to a synchronic point of view was also to be something of a return. "Linguistics," he predicted, "having accorded too large a place to history, will turn back to the static viewpoint of traditional grammar but in a new spirit and with other procedures" *(pp. 82–83)*.

Bloomfield sees it quite differently. His main objection to the study of linguistic change is not, as de Saussure's was, that its theoretical foundations are shaky but rather that because it can be carried on "only by comparing related languages or different historical stages of the same language," it led nineteenth-century linguists to ignore "languages whose history was unknown." Thus in his view it

> . . . cut them off from a knowledge of foreign types of grammatical structure, which would have opened their eyes to the fact that even the fundamental features of Indo-European grammar, such as, especially, the part-of-speech system, are by no means universal in human speech. Believing these features to be universal, they resorted, whenever they dealt with fundamentals, to philosophical and psychological pseudo-explanations. *[p. 17]*

This limitation of interest encouraged an unscientific preoccupation with "mental processes" and "philosophical speculations" which Bloomfield takes to be the nineteenth century's legacy from earlier (and even less scientific) linguists who "stated the grammatical features of language in philosophical terms and took no account of the structural difference between languages, but obscured it by forcing their descriptions into the scheme of Latin grammar" *(p. 8)*. And for him this earlier attitude is in turn the outgrowth of the still earlier practice of writing *"general grammars,* which were to demonstrate that the structure of various languages, and especially of Latin, embodies universally valid canons of logic," a practice that he says led to "the belief that the grammarian or lexicographer, fortified by his powers of reasoning, can ascertain the logical basis of language and prescribe how people ought to speak" *(pp. 6–7).* As an example of this misguided faith, Bloomfield singles out the same book de Saussure had praised as an early example of the "strictly synchronic" attempt to "describe language-states," the *Grammaire générale et raisonée* of 1660 written at the Convent of Port Royal and sometimes referred to as *The Port Royal Grammar.*

Thus while de Saussure sees nineteenth-century comparativism as representing, for all its practical successes, a theoretical falling-off, Bloomfield sees it as representing, for all its inadequacies, an unequivocal advance; and therefore he, unlike de Saussure, has no desire to return—even "in a new spirit and with other procedures"—to the viewpoint of pre-nineteenth-century linguistics. One reason for this difference is probably that American linguists, whose view of history is here fairly represented by Bloomfield, arrived by a route quite different from de Saussure's at the conviction that tracing the history of languages and comparing them with each other ought to be subordinated to accurate synchronic description. For de Saussure the shift from a diachronic to a synchronic point of view resulted, as the passages I have quoted from him suggest, from a purely theoretical concern that linguistics "delimit and define itself" *(p. 6);* but in American linguistics this same shift, which was already taking place when de Saussure was delivering at Geneva the lectures that were to become the *Course in General Linguistics,* seems rather to have resulted from the practical exigencies of describing and classifying American Indian languages. Their overriding interest in linguistic change had led most of the great nineteenth-century linguists to concentrate on languages with known histories, and therefore languages whose speakers had not developed a system of writing and which thus had no accessible histories had been left mainly to explorers and missionaries. Moreover, when such languages had been investigated, the assumption (censured by Bloomfield) that the fundamental features of Indo-European grammar are universal had evidently led the investigators to suppose that any language that does not clearly manifest these features must be to that extent unsystematic. A growing awareness that American Indian languages, despite their remoteness from the familiar civilized languages (and in fact from each other), were extremely complex and perfectly systematic forced American linguists to see the disastrous inadequacy of this view.

Therefore Franz Boas, in his 1911 introduction to the Bureau of American Ethnology's *Handbook of American Indian Languages*,[8] took great pains to show that the categories of sounds, concepts, and grammatical elements employed in describing the Indo-European languages are indeed irrelevant to the description of many American Indian languages, but that we cannot conclude from this that savages are less accurate in their pronunciation than civilized men, or that their languages either are inferior to civilized languages in conceptual power or are haphazardly structured. If (for example) the Pawnees have a single sound that at times sounds to European ears like *l* but at other times like *r* or *n* or *d*, this merely shows that the phonetic distinctions functional in our languages are not functional in all others; conversely, phonetic distinctions functional in Indian languages are often not functional in ours. "Thus, for instance," writes Boas, "the Indians of the North

[8] Smithsonian Institution, Bureau of American Ethnology, Bulletin 40, Part I (Washington, D.C.: U.S. Government Printing Office, 1911), pp. 3–83.

Pacific coast have a series of *l* sounds, which may be roughly compared to our sounds *tl, cl, gl*. Consequently, a word like *close* is heard by the Indians sometimes one way, sometimes another; our *cl* is for them an intermediate sound, in the same way as some Indian sounds are intermediate sounds to our ears" *(p. 18)*. The same is true of conceptual and grammatical distinctions. Formerly it had been thought that primitive languages were characterized by *holophrasis*, the tendency to express a complex idea by a single simple term, but since (to quote Boas again) "the selection of such simple terms must to a certain extent depend upon the chief interests of a people," and since "each language, from the point of view of another language, may be arbitrary in its classifications," therefore "every language may be holophrastic from the point of view of another language" *(p. 26)*. Finally, while an Indian language may fail to make (for example) the familiar grammatical distinctions of gender, number, and case when dealing with nouns, it may distinguish them instead by tense, or by whether they refer to animate or inanimate objects.

The primary aim of the grammatical discussions introduced by Boas' essay was thus to avoid the imposition of our familiar categories on the Indian languages. In the decades that followed, the shift from a diachronic to a synchronic point of view got firmly connected in the minds of most American linguists with the need to approach each new language in a spirit of healthy relativism, free of all inhibiting theories about the nature of language in general; conversely, they came to assume unquestioningly that such theories would necessarily inhibit the twentieth-century linguist, just as they had his eighteenth-century counterpart. As Bloomfield put it:

Students of American languages could indulge in no self-deception as to the need of descriptive data: north of Mexico alone there are dozens of totally unrelated groups of languages,

> presenting the most varied types of structure. In the stress of recording utterly strange forms of speech one soon learned that philosophical prepossessions were only a hindrance. [p. 19]

Moreover, while Bloomfield himself did believe that "when we have adequate data about many languages, we shall have to return to the problem of general grammar" (p. 20), the tendency of American linguists has increasingly been to disavow even the existence of this problem and, in their eagerness not to force remote languages into a Procrustean bed of familiar categories, to deny the very possibility of generalizing fruitfully about the nature of language. Martin Joos, for example, assumes the existence of a state of affairs that would render all such generalizing logically impossible when he refers to "the American (Boas) tradition that languages [can] differ from each other without limit and in unpredictable ways."[9] Their fierce suspicion of all theories has sometimes even led American linguists to speak of theorizing as a species of bigotry. In their standard *Outline of Linguistic Analysis*, Bernard Bloch and George L. Trager refer to the "naïve surprise" often occasioned by the discovery that not everyone in the world speaks one's own language, and they add that "some persons even go so far as to elevate the grammar of a particular language—usually Latin—to the rank of abstract reason, and to regard all deviations from this pattern in other languages as illogical corruptions." The true linguist, they sternly tell us, "will take each language as he finds it, and set himself to learning its vocabulary and grammar without the inhibiting prejudice of the bigot to whom all that is unfamiliar is absurd."[10] De Saussure, on the other hand, believed that "To synchrony belongs everything called 'general grammar'" (p. 101).

[9] Martin Joos (ed.), *Readings in Linguistics,* 2d ed. (New York: American Council of Learned Societies, 1958), p. 96.

[10] (Baltimore: Linguistic Society of America, 1942), p. 7.

Since their objections to theorizing about language are based on a fear that theories will get in the way of direct, unbiased observation of the linguistic data, it is understandable that the term American linguists have most often brought forward as the polar opposite of *theory* is *observation*. Bloomfield, for example, praises the ancient Sanskrit grammar of Pāṇini for having "presented to European eyes, for the first time, a complete and accurate description of a language, based not upon theory but upon observation" *(p. 11)*. Therefore when American linguists have felt the need to justify their discipline as a science, they have usually done so by insisting that they deal only with observable physical events or behavior and indulge in no airy speculations about unobservables, particularly about the nature or workings of the mind. Zellig Harris defines a language as "the talk which takes place in a language community" and utterances as "stretches of continuous events."[11] And W. Freeman Twaddell explains that since "we have no right to guess about the linguistic workings of an inaccessible 'mind,'" the linguist is committed (and limited) to "the study of phenomena and their correlations." "The scientific method," Twaddell adds, "is quite simply the convention that mind does not exist."[12] The general conception of science on which such justifications rest was trenchantly expressed by Bloomfield in his *Linguistic Aspects of Science*:

. . . we can distinguish science from other phases of human activity by agreeing that science shall deal only with events that are accessible in their time and place to any and all observers (strict *behaviorism*) or only with events that are placed in co-ordinates of time and space *(mechanism)*, or that science shall employ only such initial statements and predictions as lead to definite handling operations *(operationalism)*, or only terms

[11] *Methods in Structural Linguistics* (Chicago: University of Chicago Press, 1951), pp. 13 and 25.

[12] "On Defining the Phoneme," in Joos, *Readings,* p. 57.

such as are derivable by rigid definition from a set of everyday terms concerning physical happenings *(physicalism)*. These several formulations, independently reached by different scientists, all lead to the same delimitation, and this delimitation does not restrict the subject matter of science but rather characterizes its method.[13]

Bloomfield's point was that although "In the common sense of many peoples, perhaps of all, language is largely ignored, and its effects are explained as owing to nonphysical factors, the action of a 'mind,' 'will,' or the like," such terms (which he called *mentalistic* terms) "have no place in science" *(Linguistic Aspects, pp. 12–13).*

Another (and related) way in which American linguists have tried to demonstrate that their enterprise is a genuinely scientific one is by insisting that they are concerned only with *description* and not with *explanation.* "Children want explanations," writes Joos, "and there is a child in each of us; descriptivism makes a virtue of not pampering that child" *(Readings, p. 96).* After telling us that just as a community's laws "are simply an orderly description of [certain] acts and their relations," so "the grammar of a language is simply an orderly description of the way people in a given society talk" *(Outline, p. 6),* Bloch and Trager write:

To explain the facts which he has described, the linguist traces the forms of a language back through the past, and compares them with corresponding forms in related languages. In terms of linguistic science, the only answer to the question Why? is a historical statement. Why do we call an animal of the species *Equus caballus* a horse?—because that is what our parents called it, and their English-speaking ancestors before them for over a thousand years. . . . It is important to remember that linguistics can explain the facts of a language only in this way: by stating what the corresponding facts were at an

[13] (Chicago: University of Chicago Press, 1939), p. 13.

earlier stage of the language and by describing the changes that have intervened. Attempts to answer the question Why? in other ways—by appeals to psychology, philosophy, or abstract logic—may seem esthetically more satisfying, but are never anything better than guesses, unprovable and fruitless. *[pp. 8–9]*

At another point in his *Readings in Linguistics* Joos makes the point even more vehemently. Of Bloomfield he writes: "For him there was enough that demanded unambiguous statement in what we all see and hear; why borrow trouble by explaining the invisible? . . . If the facts have been fully stated, it is perverse or childish to demand an explanation into the bargain" *(p. v).*

Now this extraordinary animus against explanations as being necessarily unscientific may well seem strange to a layman, for when we learn about Boyle's law or quantum mechanics or electromagnetism it seems natural enough to say that certain important things about the physical world are being explained to us. But there is a long and important tradition in the philosophy of science which denies this: I am referring to the tradition often associated with the name "positivism," the tradition from which Bloomfield acquired the general view of science that he passed on to his colleagues. According to the positivist view, which received its classical expression in John Stuart Mill's *System of Logic* (1843) and was handed down to the twentieth century by such writers as Karl Pearson and Ernst Mach, the "laws" that scientists attempt to formulate are really extremely condensed generalizations or summaries of the behavior of natural phenomena or of our experience of their behavior: scientific laws do not explain *why* things happen as they do, but rather describe *how* they happen. Obviously then, the word "law" is used in science quite differently from the way it is used when we speak of the civil laws laid down or prescribed by some duly constituted authority. Citizens must conform to the law of the land or they will be punished, but it would make no sense to speak of requiring natural phenomena to "conform" to scientific laws. In fact it is just the other way round with scientific laws: if they are to have any scientific value, *they* must (at the very least) conform to the observed behavior of the phenomena they purport to cover.

This distinction between the two senses of the word "law" seems obvious enough to us, but it was not drawn easily. The reason it had to be drawn clearly is probably that by the middle of the nineteenth century natural science was finally detaching itself from the amalgam of science, metaphysics, and theology once called "natural philosophy." As Mill wrote, though "the expression, Laws of Nature, *means* nothing but the uniformities which exist among natural phenomena . . . when reduced to their simplest expression," yet it "has generally been employed with a sort of tacit reference to the original sense of the word law, namely, the expression of the will of a superior."[14] Since earlier, less objective and less secular accounts of the natural world had tried to reveal divine providence as the cause and end of natural order, in effect treating laws of nature rather like civil laws imposed by God, the distinction between the two kinds of law got connected with the distinction between objective description and quasi-metaphysical explanation, and then—quite misleadingly, as we shall see—with the general distinction between description and explanation. And perhaps partly for reasons of euphony, it became common to state the opposition of description to explanation as the opposition of *de*scription to *pre*scription. "The civil law involves a command and a duty; the scientific law is a description, not a prescription," wrote Pearson.[15]

[14] *System of Logic,* III, iv, 1.

[15] *The Grammar of Science* (London: Dent, 1937; 1st printing, 1892), p. 77.

And Mach (or rather his translator) was concerned about the danger that, "once the subjective aspect of our conception of nature is introduced, little seems to prevent us from taking the extreme position that our mode of perception and our concepts alone *prescribe* laws to nature."[16] Thus explanation came to be thought of as implying everything science had freed itself from at last and should at all costs seek to avoid in the future; and this implication was strengthened by the difficulties with the word "law," which connected explanation with prescription, the sovereign imposition of one's will on what apparently should be observed neutrally and objectively.

Now it had always been common to speak of rules of grammar, but since the word "rule" shares the troublesome implications of the word "law" it was natural that the application to linguistics of the positivist view of science should lead linguists to insist not only that they were merely describing (rather than explaining) but also that in so doing they were not specifying *rules* but rather what Mill called uniformities and they often call *regularities*—those "correlations" of "phenomena" to which Twaddell refers. In *Methods in Structural Linguistics*, usually regarded as the clearest and most comprehensive exposition of the methods evolved by American linguists for investigating linguistic structure, Zellig Harris defines descriptive linguistics as

. . . a particular field of inquiry which deals not with the whole of speech activities, but with the regularities in certain features of speech. These regularities are in the distributional relations

---

[16] "The Significance and Purpose of Natural Laws," Frederic Shick (trans.), in Arthur Danto and Sidney Morgenbesser (eds.), *Philosophy of Science* (Cleveland: World Publishing, 1960), p. 266 In German the describe–prescribe distinction is marked by the two words *"beschreiben"* and *"vorschreiben,"* respectively; for the original of the Mach passage, see his *Erkenntnis und Irrtum* (Leipzig: Verlag von Johann Ambrosius Barth, 1905), p. 441.

among the features of speech in question, i.e. the occurrence of these features relatively to each other within utterances. . . . The main research of descriptive linguistics, and the only relation which will be accepted as relevant in the present survey, is the distribution or arrangement within the flow of speech of some parts or features relatively to others. [p. 5]

The resulting conception of linguistic method is that the linguist, starting from "the flow of speech," the physical events that make up his stock or corpus of utterances, successively erects classes of significant sounds (*phonemes*), classes of phoneme-sequences (*morphemes*), and classes of morpheme-sequences (*constituents*). At no point does he introduce anything other than physical events or make any assumptions about what Twaddell called "the workings of an inaccessible 'mind.' " "The basic operations," Harris tells us, "are segmentation and classification" (*Methods*, p. 367), which "yield various sets of linguistic elements, at various levels of analysis" (p. 364), each new element being "defined by the relations among elements at the next lower level" (p. 369). The end product is a grammar, a description of the structure of the language under investigation; such a description, which constitutes "a compact one-one representation of the stock of utterances in the corpus" (p. 366), can in Harris' view "be presented most baldly in an ordered set of statements defining the elements at each successive level or stating the sequences which occur at that level" (p. 373).

We now have an answer to the second of our two questions, as applied to American descriptive or structural linguistics: the structure of a language does not reflect or picture the structure of the world or of anything else but is rather the particular set of linguistic elements and levels represented by the grammar, a hierarchial pattern that emerges from the linguist's study of the verbal behavior of the speakers of the language just as the pattern represented by those classificatory hierarchies in introductory zoology texts emerges from a study of the animal kingdom.

But what about our other question: How do these same linguists conceive of meanings, and what sort of thing do they take them to be? Perhaps the first thing to be said is that while it isn't quite fair to charge, as some writers have done, that Bloomfield and his followers unconditionally banished the study of meaning from linguistics, it does seem fair to say that they swept it under the rug, for their treatments of meaning have invariably been vague and sketchy. Given their conception of linguistic structure as a pattern of behavioral regularities, it is not hard to see why this should be so. For while the behavioral regularities relevant to the study of phonology and syntax, the two branches of grammar as it is usually conceived of by American linguists, are regularities that hold among elements or sequences of elements within the system of the language, the regularities relevant to the study of meaning would seem to be those that hold between words or utterances and something outside the language—objects or situations or ideas, perhaps. Therefore it is no surprise that Bloomfield defines the meaning of an utterance or linguistic form as "the situation in which the speaker utters it and the response which it calls forth in the hearer" (*Language, p. 139*), or that Archibald Hill, writing twenty-five years later, says that "Meaning proper is ultimately correspondence between a linguistic item and an item in the nonsymbolic world, or between a linguistic structure of many items and a similar structure in the nonsymbolic world."[17] Nor is it any surprise that this assumed need to go outside the system of the language should have made American linguists feel that any appeal to meaning made in studying phonology or syntax would inevitably result in a loss of the rigor

[17] *Introduction to Linguistic Structures* (New York: Harcourt Brace Jovanovich, 1958), p. 410.

possible so long as one stays within that system, and that the study of meaning itself would require the acquisition of so much new non-linguistic knowledge as to render it scientifically impracticable. Harris warns us that "In exact descriptive linguistic work . . . considerations of meaning can only be used heuristically, as a source of hints, and the determining criteria will always have to be stated in distributional terms" *(Methods, p. 365, n. 6)*. And Bloomfield, immediately after his definition of meaning, adds:

> In order to give a scientifically accurate definition of meaning for every form of a language, we should have to have a scientifically accurate knowledge of everything in the speakers' world. The actual extent of human knowledge is very small, compared to this. . . . The statement of meanings is therefore the weak point in language-study, and will remain so until human knowledge advances very far beyond its present state. *[Language, pp. 139–140]*

Thus American linguists have tended to regard semantics suspiciously, as lying beyond the pale, incapable of investigation by the rigorous procedures that have worked so well in phonology and syntax. Moreover, as Bloomfield's equation of meanings with situations and responses suggests, when they have tried to go a little further and indicate what form a science of meaning might possibly take, American linguists have been led to make the first of Korzybski's two mistakes, that of confusing meanings with extralinguistic entities. A page after the pessimistic statement I just quoted, Bloomfield, using the word "apple" as his example, does try to compromise by distinguishing between "*non-distinctive* features of the situation, such as the size, shape, color, and so on of any one particular apple, and the *distinctive*, or *linguistic meaning* (the *semantic* features) which are common to all the situations that call forth the utterance of the linguistic form, such as the features which are common to all the objects of which English-speaking people use the word *apple" (Language, p. 141)*. But he does not use this distinction to extend or clarify his views on meaning, and his discussion soon trails off into a catalogue of differences in usage as determined by social class, experience, and other factors. Nor, so far as I know, has any other descriptive or structural linguist had any better success with these matters. But in the last ten years or so the course of American linguistics has been radically altered by new developments which seem to have opened up new (and more fruitful) ways of viewing and carrying on the scientific study of meaning. It is to these developments that we must turn now.

II

The book that initiated them was a short technical monograph by Noam Chomsky called *Syntactic Structures*.[18] To some linguists at least, Chomsky's main point seemed to be that a new linguistic level, which he called the transformational level, should be added to those proposed by American linguists—the phonemic, morphemic, and constituent levels. He argued that the customary way of analyzing the syntactic structure of sentences, in terms of their phrase structure, works well only for short, simple, active declarative sentences. When phrase structure analysis is extended beyond these sentences—to passive sentences, for example, or to questions—the descriptions it produces are often, as Chomsky showed, extremely complex and clumsy. Moreover, there are important relations that hold between the sentences which lend themselves to phrase structure analysis (called kernel sentences by Chomsky) and the others which do not. For example, to the kernel

[18] (The Hague: Mouton, 1957). See Robert B. Lees's review in *Language,* XXXIII (1957), 375–408.

sentence "John is reading the book" there corresponds a passive sentence ("The book is being read by John") and a number of questions ("Is John reading the book?" "What is John reading?" "Who is reading the book?"). In order to show such relations in the grammar and in order to avoid the complexities of a thorough-going phrase structure analysis (if indeed such an analysis should turn out even to be possible), Chomsky proposed that only the kernel sentences be accounted for directly in terms of phrase structure and that the others be viewed as derived from the kernel sentences by operations which he called transformations.

But Chomsky was actually proposing changes far more extensive than the mere addition of the transformational level to the conception of linguistic structure evolved by American linguists. After all, if we take literally Harris' description of a grammar as "a compact one-one representation of the stock of utterances in the corpus," the complexities that result from phrase structure analysis, and its failure to show the relations between kernel sentences and their transforms, are not necessarily defects; therefore the motivation for adding the transformational level vanishes. Chomsky was writing not only with a view of linguistic structure different from that of other American linguists but also with a quite different general conception of the scope and nature of his subject—a conception, I might add, that has become a good deal clearer to an outsider like myself in the books and essays that he and his colleagues have written since *Syntactic Structures*.[19] De Saussure has had so powerful an influence in shaping this conception that one way of considering Chomsky's work is as an attempt to incorporate the practical achievements of American linguistics within a more precise and workable formulation of de Saussure's theoretical views; therefore

[19] Many of these essays are collected in Jerry A. Fodor and Jerrold J. Katz (eds.), *The Structure of Language* (Englewood Cliffs, N.J.: Prentice-Hall, 1964).

it will be helpful at this point to examine a little further the differences between those views and Bloomfield's.

His concern that linguistics "delimit and define itself" led de Saussure to the same conclusion reached by the American linguists who were to follow him and (tentatively at least) to claim him as a forerunner: that in order to be a real science linguistics must have a clearly specified object open to empirical investigation. And he, like them, saw the rejection of the nineteenth century's concern with history as an important step towards attaining this goal. But whereas the American linguists came to feel that such an object must be strictly limited to the physical events that make up observable speech behavior, his view was just the opposite. For he made his distinction between synchronic and diachronic linguistics within the context of another (and logically prior) distinction between language proper (which he called *langue*) and mere speaking or speech behavior (*parole*). It was only after he had established the study of *langue* as the only sort of linguistics capable of becoming a real science that he went on to distinguish, within that study, between synchrony and diachrony, and to stress the predominance of the former. To clarify the relation of *langue* to *parole* he compared it to the relation of a symphony to its performances: "what the symphony actually is stands completely apart from how it is performed; the mistakes that musicians make in playing the symphony do not compromise this fact" (*p. 18*). And he recommended that linguists ignore *parole*, which he said was merely "the sum of what people say" and thus "not a collective instrument; its manifestations are individual and momentary" (*p. 19*). The reason he thought *langue* was the object linguistics demanded, "a well-defined object in the heterogeneous mass of speech facts," was thus precisely that it was *not* observable behavior but rather "a grammatical system that has a potential existence in each brain, or, more specifically, in the brains of a group of individuals" *(pp. 13–14)*.

De Saussure's reasons for stressing the predominance of synchronic study are therefore quite different from Bloomfield's. Bloomfield, whose view we may again fairly take as representative of American descriptive linguists, writes:

All historical study of language is based upon the comparison of two or more sets of descriptive data. It can be only as accurate and only as complete as these data permit it to be. In order to describe a language one needs no historical knowledge whatever; in fact, the observer who allows such knowledge to affect his description, is bound to distort his data. Our descriptions must be unprejudiced, if they are to give a sound basis for comparative work. *[Language, pp. 19–20]*

But de Saussure's claims are much stronger:

The first thing that strikes us when we study the facts of language is that their succession in time does not exist insofar as the speaker is concerned. He is confronted with a state. That is why the linguist who wishes to understand a state must discard all knowledge of everything that produced it and ignore diachrony. He can enter the mind of speakers only by completely suppressing the past. The intervention of history can only falsify his judgment. It would be absurd to attempt to sketch a panorama of the Alps by viewing them simultaneously from several peaks of the Jura; a panorama must be made from a single vantage point. The same applies to language; the linguist can neither describe it nor draw up standards of usage except by concentrating on one state. When he follows the evolution of the language, he resembles the moving observer who goes from one peak of the Jura to another in order to record the shifts in perspective. *[pp. 81–82]*

In direct contrast to Bloomfield, de Saussure does not believe that "science shall deal only with events that are accessible in their time and place to any and all observers," but rather takes it for granted that if linguistics is to be a real science the linguist must "enter the mind of speakers" and attempt to discover the precise nature of the mental or psychological reality—not itself directly accessible to observation—which somehow underlies, and must be postulated to explain, the "individual and momentary" manifestations of *parole*. This mental or psychological reality is the object de Saussure calls *langue*, and since it can only be postulated as existing at a given moment in time to explain a given "language-state," he believes that "the synchronic viewpoint predominates" not simply because historical information is unnecessary in describing a language and may distort or prejudice the description but rather because "it [i.e., the synchronic viewpoint] is the true and only reality to the community of speakers" *(p. 90)*.

Now Chomsky agrees with de Saussure, and disagrees with Bloomfield and most American linguists, as to the general goals of linguistics.[20] In attempting to arrive at a clearer formulation of de Saussure's view than de Saussure himself managed to provide, Chomsky has drawn not only on the practical achievements of American linguistics but also on his own knowledge of the philosophy of science and of the methods of the more advanced sciences, as well as on recent work in psychology and the foundations of mathematics.

In the first place, Chomsky has taken issue with the general conception of science common to most American linguists by laying his stress on theory construction and validation rather than on the collection and classification of data. He has argued that since the observed data and the regularities holding among them are not regarded by physicists or chemists as

[20] But in conceiving of a grammar as a system of rules (see below, pp. 83 ff.), Chomsky differs from de Saussure. See Chomsky, *Current Issues in Linguistic Theory* (The Hague: Mouton, 1964), p. 23, and *Aspects of the Theory of Syntax* (Cambridge, Mass.: M.I.T. Press, 1965), p. 4. The former passage may also be found in *The Structure of Language*, pp. 59–60.

ends in themselves but rather as means to a further end, as evidence on the basis of which one may form and test theories that attempt to explain facts lying beyond the data, the same must be true in linguistics if it is to be genuinely scientific. Invoking a phrase of Harris' that I quoted earlier, Chomsky once wrote:

> The linguist's data consist of certain observations about the form and use of utterances. The facts of linguistic structure that he hopes to discover go well beyond these observations. A grammar of a particular language is, in effect, an hypothesis about the principles of sentence formation in this language. It represents a factual claim concerning the rules that underlie the data that have been collected. . . . A grammatical description that gives nothing more than "a compact one-one representation of the stock of utterances in the corpus" can be challenged only to the extent that the observations it summarizes or rearranges are defective. It claims little, and its interest is correspondingly limited.[21]

And again: "Gross coverage of many facts can undoubtedly be obtained in many different ways. What we want in a grammar is not mere coverage of facts, but insightful coverage, something much more difficult to define or to attain."[22] Thus the claims that Bloomfieldian linguists have made in their theoretical pronouncements—that they confine themselves to classifying physical events, that they make no assumptions about the mind and its workings, that they are interested in observation rather than theory and in description rather than explanation—seem to Chomsky to embody precisely the sort of arbitrary and artificial self-limitation which would keep linguistics or any other study from ever becoming a science.

In attempting to give a more precise characteriza-

<hr />

[21] "Some Methodological Remarks on Grammar," *Word,* XVII (1961), 219–220.

[22] "Explanatory Models in Linguistics," in E. Nagel, P. Suppes, and A. Tarski (eds.), *Logic, Methodology and Philosophy of Science* (Stanford, Cal.: Stanford University Press, 1962), p. 549.

tion of the underlying reality that de Saussure called *langue*, Chomsky has started from the assumption that the most important and baffling aspect of our use of language, and therefore the one most in need of explanation, is what he calls *creativity*:

> The central fact to which any significant linguistic theory must address itself is this: a mature speaker can produce a new sentence of his language on the appropriate occasion, and other speakers can understand it immediately, though it is equally new to them. Most of our linguistic experience, both as speakers and hearers, is with new sentences; once we have mastered a language, the class of sentences with which we can operate fluently and without difficulty or hesitation is so vast that for all practical purposes (and, obviously, for all theoretical purposes), we may regard it as infinite. [*Current Issues, p. 7*]

Since we attain this creative ability to deal with an infinite number of sentences on the basis of (necessarily) finite experience, language must be somehow systematic or rule-governed, in order to provide us with the means of extrapolating from finite to infinite. As Chomsky has put it, "the learnability of language forces us to assume that it is governed by some kinds of rules. When we learn our native language we make some very complicated inductions. If these inductions are systematic, it follows that language is systematic."[23] Moreover, since the psychological facts of language-learning make it clear that this ability is not only attained on the basis of finite experience but is also attained—at quite an early age and by all normal human beings, intelligent and stupid alike—on the basis of experience that is really extraordinarily limited and fragmentary, Chomsky has

[23] Archibald Hill (ed.), *Third Texas Conference on Problems of Linguistic Analysis in English* (Austin, Texas: University of Texas, 1962), p. 181. Since this passage occurs in a discussion following Chomsky's paper, "A Transformational Approach to Syntax," it is not reprinted with that paper in *The Structure of Language*.

concluded that the rules governing it must be extraordinarily powerful and general. To quote again:

> . . . the relative suddenness, uniformity, and universality of language learning, the bewildering complexity of the resulting skills, and the subtlety and finesse with which they are exercised, all point to the conclusion that a primary and essential factor is the contribution of an organism with highly intricate and specific initial structure. ["Explanatory Models," p. 536]

The system of rules which this structure enables each of us to internalize in the process of learning his language is the reality that Chomsky thinks the linguist seeks to describe.

As Chomsky has often pointed out, this interest in linguistic creativity is not new; in fact he has been at pains to trace its historical lineage in order to insist that although his work has sometimes been viewed as being "in some way an outgrowth of attempts to use electronic computers for one or another purpose, . . . in fact . . . its roots are firmly in traditional linguistics (Current Issues, p. 25).[24] Yet the technical means to formulate this traditional interest precisely have not been made available until recently, as a result of the work in the foundations of mathematics that I referred to above. Without getting into the important but difficult technicalities of this work and

[24] See Chomsky's *Aspects of the Theory of Syntax*, pp. 3–9 and 47–52; *Cartesian Linguistics* (New York: Harper & Row, 1966) and *Language and Mind* (New York: Harcourt Brace Jovanovich, 1968), *passim;* and "Linguistics and Philosophy," in Sidney Hook (ed.), *Language and Philosophy* (New York: New York University Press, 1969), pp. 51–94. For criticism of Chomsky's treatment of earlier thinkers in these works, see Gilbert Harman's review of *Cartesian Linguistics,* in *The Philosophical Review,* LXXVII (1968), 229–235; and Hans Aarsleff, "The History of Linguistics and Professor Chomsky," *Language,* XLVI (1970), 570–585. For criticism of Chomsky's philosophical position see J. M. E. Moravcsik, "Linguistic Theory and the Philosophy of Language," *Foundations of Language,* III (1967), 209–233; the other articles in Part II of the Hook volume; and D. W. Hamlyn's review of *Language and Mind,* in *Metaphilosophy,* I (1970), 268–272.

its applications to linguistics—technicalities that I am completely incompetent to deal with—we can easily see that mathematics is at least potentially useful in dealing with the problem of linguistic creativity since it offers examples of finite sets of rules that implicitly specify or enumerate infinite sets of objects.[25] Just as we do not (and could not) learn a language merely by learning a list of sentences but rather by learning a system of rules, so too we learn ordinary arithmetic not merely by memorizing lists of numbers and their sums or products but also by learning rules. And just as we are in a position to use or understand an infinite number of sentences once we have mastered the rules of a language, so we are in a position to produce an infinite number of integers once we have mastered the rules of arithmetic, for by applying those rules to a given integer we can always produce a larger one.

Of course in actual life we don't use the rules of arithmetic to go on producing larger and larger numbers any more than we use the rules of language to produce longer and ever longer sentences—our memories and lifetimes are limited, and we have other things to do. But the point brought out by the analogy is precisely that such limitations of memory and lifetime are as irrelevant to the linguist as to the mathematician. That is, we have no more reason to expect the linguist to take such limitations into account in specifying the rules of a language than we should to require (in Chomsky's words) "that the rules of arithmetic be formulated so as to reflect precisely the ability of a human to perform calculations correctly in his head."[26] And there are many other things

[25] For a brief untechnical explanation, see Paul M. Postal, "Underlying and Superficial Linguistic Structure," *Harvard Educational Review*, XXXIV (1964), 246–249.

[26] "On the Notion 'Rule of Grammar,'" in *Structure of Language and Its Mathematical Aspects,* Proceedings of Symposia in Applied Mathematics, XII (Providence, R.I.: American Mathematical Society, 1961), p. 8.

about the way we actually speak that we have no reason to expect the linguist to take into account. As anyone who has ever tape-recorded a spontaneous conversation knows, our ordinary linguistic performance is full of sloppily pronounced words, fragmentary and ungrammatical sentences, false starts, lapses, and so on. But these are merely phonological and syntactic accidents: when we produce them we are not applying the rules of our language precisely but slightly misapplying them, not just exercising our competence in our language but slightly abusing it as well. Similarly, when somebody else understands us in spite of such accidents, he is using not only his linguistic knowledge but other knowledge as well. Such accidents are thus of no interest to the linguist.

Chomsky's usual way of making de Saussure's point about *langue* and *parole* is in fact to say that the linguist is interested in our linguistic *competence* rather than our linguistic *performance*, in our intuitive knowledge of our language rather than in precisely how that knowledge emerges in practice. Just as a mathematician studies abstract or ideal objects like numbers and geometrical figures rather than marks on blackboards or on pieces of paper, so too the linguist studies objects like sentences, idealizations that abstract away from the linguistically irrelevant aspects of actual physical utterances. Therefore the grammar he produces will (in Chomsky's words) be "an idealization in at least two respects: first, in that it considers formal structure independently of use; and second, in that the items that it generates will not be the utterances of which actual discourse is composed, but rather they will be what the untutored native speaker knows to be well-formed sentences" (*"Explanatory Models," p. 531*). To the charge, once made in discussion by Archibald Hill, that he is "not studying language at all, but some form of psychology, the intuitions of native speakers," Chomsky's reply was simply: "That is studying language. . . . I believe that native-speaker intuitions are what everyone stud-ies" *(Third Texas Conference, p. 167)*.

Finally, Chomsky also agrees with de Saussure (and disagrees with most American linguists) in wanting to reopen the large general questions about the nature of language which the seventeenth and eighteenth centuries had asked and the nineteenth had for the most part set aside. Since all natural human languages are learned with equal facility as first languages by normal children, Chomsky reasons that all languages must have the same general form, and hence that Joos cannot be right in saying that they "differ from each other without limit and in unpredictable ways." Just as the job of a linguist studying a particular language is to specify the system of rules that explains and cor-rectly predicts the linguistic intuitions of a native speaker and thus characterizes his knowledge of the language, so for Chomsky the goal of grammatical theory (or "general grammar") is to specify the general form of grammars and thus to characterize systemati-cally the innate intellectual equipment that every normal child brings to the job of learning his lan-guage—what de Saussure called the *faculté de lan-gage*. Needless to say, this goal is extremely remote.

Before we go on to attempt answers to our two initial questions as they apply to Chomsky's revised version of American linguistics—that is, to summarize his notion of linguistic structure and to see how he conceives of meanings—it will be helpful to consider two important objections to his views. The first of these is that by taking the linguistic knowledge or intuitions of native speakers as what the linguist tries to characterize, and in fact by bringing mental capaci-ties or processes into linguistics at all, Chomsky is placing the linguist in the dilemma of having either to make unscientific (and even supernaturalist) as-sumptions about the relation of mind to matter, or else to do psychology or neurology rather than lin-guistics.

In a passage in *Language* that anticipates the remarks of Twaddell's I quoted above, Bloomfield distinguished between "two theories about human conduct, including speech" *(p. 32)*, which he called the *materialistic* and *mentalistic* theories, and he asserted that "in all sciences like linguistics, which observe some specific type of human activity, the worker must proceed exactly as if he held the materialistic view" *(p. 38)*:

Human actions, according to the materialistic view, are part of cause-and-effect sequences exactly like those which we observe, say in the study of physics or chemistry, . . . [whereas the mentalistic view] supposes that the variability of human conduct is due to the interference of some non-physical factor, a *spirit* or *will* or *mind* . . . that is present in every human being. This spirit, according to the mentalistic view, is entirely different from material things and accordingly follows some other kind of causation or perhaps none at all. *[pp. 33 and 32]*

Therefore, Bloomfield reasoned, causal explanation will be impossible for the linguist who adopts the mentalistic view.

Of course such a linguist still has the alternative of adopting the materialistic view but retaining his conviction that the proper aim of linguistics is to formulate the principles of mental operation underlying a native speaker's use of his language rather than merely to establish the regularities that hold among the utterances of his corpus. But as Hill suggests by commenting that Chomsky is "not studying language at all, but some form of psychology," if the linguist chooses this alternative he would seem to be committed to the view that anything he says about mental capacities or processes could (and really should) be translated into statements about some sort of bodily processes; and of course if he attempts such a translation he will wind up in some field other than linguistics.

This objection has been met very persuasively by Jerrold Katz in an essay called "Mentalism in Lin-

Cohen, has blamed the tendency of ordinary language philosophers to talk about rules on their ignorance of linguistics, and specifically on their ignorance of the fact that while the word "rule" does sometimes occur "in connection with word-use in the professional writings of modern descriptive and historical linguists," it "is generally otiose or misleading in such contexts—a mere synonym for 'regularity' or 'uniformity.' "[29] After contrasting two sorts of approaches to language, de facto approaches that consider a language as "a pattern of events" and de jure approaches that consider it as "a system of rules" *(p. 24)*, Cohen asserts that the latter sort has been rejected by modern linguists as necessarily prescriptive or normative and adds that "from a descriptive or historical point of view every dialect, Cockney no less than standard English, has its own grammar even if this grammar is not taught in elementary schools" *(p. 37)*.

This objection has been answered by J. A. Fodor in a penetrating review of Cohen's book.[30] Cohen's contrast of de facto and de jure approaches is misdirected, Fodor argues:

The general point is this: *rule theories are not to be contrasted with regularity theories, since rules are invoked in linguistics precisely in order to account for what regularities are known to obtain.* That is, a paradigmatic form of explanation in linguistics is: "this regularity can be accounted for on the assumption that speakers are following this rule." Hence, a linguistic theory articulated in terms of regularities to the exclusion of rules would offer data without offering explanations; conversely, a linguistic theory articulated in terms of rules to the exclusion of regularities would offer explanations that fail to be explanations of anything. I take it to be obvious that an account of linguistic theories that, in effect, permits such theories to offer either explanations or data but not both is, *ipso facto*, unsatisfactory.

[29] *The Diversity of Meaning* (London: Methuen, 1962), p. 32.
[30] *The Journal of Philosophy*, LXI (1964), 334–343.

To take an analogous case, it is immediately evident that the following proposal is senseless: "Let us distinguish between two sorts of physical theories, one of which is articulated solely in terms of regularities and the other of which is articulated solely in terms of laws." It is clear that any attempt to assign these sorts of physical theories to their appropriate domains, however ingeniously carried out, would be a waste of effort. There cannot be two such kinds of theories, since a very large part of the point of talking about physical laws is to make it possible to account in a systematic way for physical regularities and a very large part of the point of collecting data on physical regularities is to provide evidence about what physical laws there are. [pp. 340–341]

Granting that "Cohen is certainly right in arguing that the view that BBC English 'has its own grammar' is fully compatible with the view that Cockney does too," Fodor goes on to point out that

. . . that fact is itself compatible with a descriptive approach to language even where a grammar is thought of as a system of rules for producing sentences. Our attitude becomes normative only when we argue further that the rules for speaking BBC English are somehow preferable to the rules for speaking Cockney English; viz., that the former rules are the ones that ought to be adopted. [p. 342]

Cohen's mistake here, Fodor argues, is his assumption that all rules express norms. Fodor counters this assumption by calling attention to a distinction that the philosopher John Searle had drawn between two sorts of rules, *regulative* rules (like the rules of etiquette) that "regulate antecedently existing forms of behaviour" and *constitutive* rules (like the rules of football) that "do not merely regulate but create or define new forms of behavior."[31] Since regulative rules com-

---

[31] "What is a Speech Act?," in Max Black (ed.), *Philosophy in America* (London: Allen and Unwin, 1965), p. 223; the earlier date of Fodor's review is accounted for by the fact that in writing it he had access to a mimeographed version of Searle's paper. The section on rules may now also be found in Searle's book *Speech Acts* (Cambridge: Cambridge University Press, 1969), pp. 33–42.

monly take the form of imperatives, they can indeed be said to express norms; but since constitutive rules commonly take the form of definitions or tautologies, they cannot. Fodor then points out that in speaking of a grammar as a system of rules, Chomsky is thinking of constitutive rather than regulative rules and therefore is not open to the charge of being prescriptive or normative. That is, rules of grammar as Chomsky conceives them do not (for example) command us to use one sentence rather than another as the rules of etiquette command us to wear a black tie or an evening gown on certain occasions; rather they define concepts like *sentence of English* by generating all (and only) the sentences of English, just as the rule specifying the conditions for scoring a touchdown defines the concept *touchdown* by telling us just which actions are to count as a touchdown.

I think this distinction is an extremely important one. Not that it solves all the difficulties about what a rule of language is—as Fodor points out at the end of his review, we are still left with the problem of explaining how there can be rules "which govern the behavior of speakers but which they are unaware of employing and unable to formulate," and how it is that children "internalize rules of formidable abstractness . . . without ever encountering an explicit statement of the rules they learn" *(p. 343)*. In these ways rules of language, as they figure in Chomsky's system, would seem to be different not only from the rules of football but also from the rules of multiplication. Yet Searle's distinction does clarify not only Chomsky's aims but also the strenuous objections of his American predecessors to "explanation." Bloomfield, we recall, objected to "the belief that the grammarian or lexicographer, fortified by his powers of reasoning, can ascertain the logical basis of language and prescribe how people ought to speak." Now Chomsky is in a sense trying precisely to "ascertain the logical basis of language"—though not, of course, fortified only by his own "powers of reasoning" but also by a great deal of psychological and linguistic evidence—yet, as Fodor implies, the issue of prescriptivism is irrelevant. I think that in Bloomfield's easy linkage of such attempts with attempts to "prescribe how people ought to speak," and in his apparent assumption that to do one thing is necessarily to do the other, we can see just the confusion about rules which Searle so neatly disentangles.

Having examined these two objections and the answers to them given by two of Chomsky's best known co-workers, we are in a better position to summarize his conception of linguistic structure and to set it in relation to that of linguists like Harris. For while at first it might seem that the structure of a language, to Chomsky as to Bloomfieldian descriptive linguists, is a hierarchial pattern of behavioral regularities, slightly altered by the addition of the transformational level, by now it should be clear that this is not true. Since Chomsky conceives of a grammar not as an ordered inventory of linguistic elements and levels representing the regularities that emerge from the verbal behavior of the language's speakers but rather as a system of rules representing their linguistic knowledge, the structure of a language is for him the system of abstract principles that must be postulated to account for the particular behavioral regularities that the linguist discovers. We are now ready to see what part the study of meaning plays in Chomsky's work.

III

If you assume that the linguist's proper object is the intuitive linguistic knowledge that underlies verbal behavior rather than the behavior itself, then semantics immediately becomes a more important part of linguistics, for the knowledge of what words mean (and of how they work in combination) is obviously a very important part of a fluent speaker's knowledge of his language. As Jerrold Katz, who has done more than anyone else to extend Chomsky's ideas to semantics, puts it: "If a person had a knowledge only of the phonological and syntactic structure of English, its sentences would seem to him much like lines of Lewis Carroll's 'Jabberwocky.' "[32] Before seeing how semanticists working within Chomsky's conception of linguistics have tried to systematize the knowledge that makes sentences of ordinary English different from lines of "Jabberwocky," recall for a moment what went wrong with Bloomfield's treatment of meaning. Of course Bloomfield, as we saw, drops the subject fairly quickly—though he gives it more attention than most of his followers—but we can use Hayakawa, who shares Bloomfield's conception of science but is undaunted by the difficulties it creates for a study of meaning and who therefore provides us with a convenient *reductio ad absurdum* of Bloomfield's position.

Since it is natural for anyone looking at the way words are used in actual situations to be struck by the extraordinary range of overtones with which different people will use the same word or by the fact that they will use it to refer to different objects, and since these sorts of differences are often what cause the disagreements and misunderstandings that general semantics seeks to clear up, we are not surprised when Hayakawa tells us that "the contexts of an utterance determine its meaning," and therefore:

. . . since no two contexts are ever *exactly* the same, no two meanings can ever be exactly the same. . . . To insist dogmatically that we know what a word means *in advance of its utterance* is nonsense. All we can know in advance is *approximately* what it will mean. . . . Interpretation *must* be based, therefore, on the

[32] "Semantic Theory and the Meaning of 'Good,' " *The Journal of Philosophy*, LXI (1964), 741.

totality of contexts. If it were otherwise, we should not be able to account for the fact that even if we fail to use the right (customary) words in some situations, people can very frequently understand us.

To illustrate this, he gives three examples. First he argues that since the three sentences "I believe in you," "I believe in democracy," and "I believe in Santa Claus" can be paraphrased (respectively) as "I have confidence in you," "I accept the principles implied by the term democracy," and "It is my opinion that Santa Claus exists," the phrase "believe in" has a different meaning in each of them. Next he says that when two different people use the word "kettle," its "intensional meanings" for each of them will be "the common characteristics of all the kettles he remembers." Finally he says that if four different people use the phrase "my typewriter," "we would have to point to four different typewriters to get the extensional meaning in each case," and he adds: "Also, if John says 'my typewriter' today, and again 'my typewriter' tomorrow, the extensional meaning is different in the two cases, because the typewriter is not exactly the same from one day to the next (nor from one minute to the next): slow processes of wear, change, and decay are going on constantly."[33]

Now this all sounds very tough-minded, skeptical, and cautious, and therefore has a vague air of "science" about it. But aside from the fact that to fall back on "the totality of contexts" (whatever that may be) is to put yourself in a still worse position than Bloomfield's—the very position, in fact, that Bloomfield was trying to stay out of by drawing his distinction between the distinctive and nondistinctive features of a situation—one wants to object that there is a simple and obvious intuitive sense in which Hayakawa's three expressions *do* mean the same thing from

[33] *Language in Thought and Action*, rev. ed. (New York: Harcourt Brace Jovanovich, 1964), pp. 60–62.

occasion to occasion and person to person, the sense in which (for example) "bank" does not mean the same thing in "I robbed a bank" as it does in "I sat on the bank of the river." In fact, if there were not some such sense in which their meanings remained fixed, what would be the point of Hayakawa's distinctions and how would he draw them? That Hayakawa senses this is shown by the careful stress he lays on the words *"exactly"* and *"approximately"*—the implication being that the same word or expression will at least mean approximately (if not exactly) the same thing twice, regardless of its linguistic or non-linguistic contexts, and therefore that its meanings in different contexts will at least be similar to (though not identical with) each other. But merely to say (or still worse, merely to imply) that two or more things are similar and then to leave it at that is to say nothing at all, for anything can be thought of as similar to anything else in some respect or other. What we want to know is in what respect the things in question are similar, and this Hayakawa doesn't tell us.

Moreover, when we recall the goals Chomsky set for linguistics, it becomes apparent that if we try to formulate a theory of meaning which will help in achieving those goals, what should interest us is not the differences in meaning that so interest Hayakawa but precisely the respect in which the meaning of a word or expression may be said to remain stable or fixed from one occasion or person to another. For if we want to characterize the semantic side of a fluent speaker's knowledge of his language, what we must account for is his ability to understand and communicate with other speakers. Therefore we will not be interested in situations in which we use the wrong word and are understood anyway or in situations in which we use the right word and are misunderstood. This is not because such situations are statistically rarer than normal situations in which we use the right word and are understood (though they probably are), but rather because they are semantic accidents, features of performance not of competence. In this they are on a par with the phonological and syntactic accidents I mentioned earlier. Since what we want to specify is precisely the sense of meaning in which a fluent speaker may be said to "know what a word means *in advance of its utterance*," for our purposes— and, as Bloomfield seems to have realized, for any general treatment of meaning that we could reasonably expect to get anywhere—Hayakawa begs all the interesting questions.

What has enabled linguists working within Chomsky's conception of linguistics to begin to answer these questions is their extension to semantics of his insight that linguistics has scientific interest only insofar as it abstracts away from behavior or performance to study what is admittedly an idealization, the structure of the language viewed in isolation from performance and conceived of as the system of rules which constitutes a speaker's linguistic competence. In a long and technical essay called "The Structure of a Semantic Theory,"[34] Katz and Fodor, after observing that "semantics takes over the explanation of the speaker's ability to produce and understand new sentences at the point where grammar leaves off," write:

> Grammars seek to describe the structure of a sentence *in isolation from its possible settings in linguistic discourse (written or verbal) or in nonlinguistic contexts (social or physical)*. The justification which permits the grammarian to study sentences in abstraction from the settings in which they have occurred or might occur is simply that the fluent speaker is able to construct and recognize syntactically well-formed sentences without recourse to information about settings, and this ability is what a grammar undertakes to reconstruct. . . .
> We may generalize to arrive at a sufficient condition for deter-

---

[34] *Language,* XXXIX (1963), 170–210. Reprinted in *The Structure of Language,* pp. 479–518.

mining when an ability of speakers is the proper subject matter of a synchronic theory in linguistics. The generalization is this: *If speakers possess an ability that enables them to apprehend the structure of any sentence in the infinite set of sentences of a language without reference to information about settings and without significant variation from speaker to speaker, then that ability is properly the subject matter of a synchronic theory in linguistics.*

The first question in determining the subject matter of a semantic theory is: Can we find an ability which satisfies the antecedent of this generalization, which is beyond the range of grammatical description, and which is semantic in some reasonable sense? If we can, then that ability falls within the domain of a semantic theory. *[pp. 172–174]*

In order to show that there are indeed many linguistic skills that do not fall within the province of grammar and that we can apply to a given sentence in isolation from any possible linguistic or nonlinguistic context, they imagine an artificial situation in which a speaker of English receives a single English sentence in an anonymous letter. If the sentence is "The bill is large," for example, he will recognize it as *ambiguous* since "bill" can mean either a bird's beak or a document demanding payment of a debt; "The bill is large but need not be paid," on the other hand, he will recognize as unambiguous *(pp. 174–175)*. Similarly, he will recognize that "The paint is silent" is somehow *anomalous* in a way that "The paint is wet" is not, and that "There are two chairs in the room" and "There are at least two things in the room and each is a chair" are *paraphrases* of each other while "The ball was hit by the man" and "The ball was hit" are not *(p. 175)*. Thus they conclude that the general ability comprising such skills, which they call simply *the ability to interpret sentences*, is the ability a semantic theory must characterize.

The pessimistic statement quoted earlier from Bloomfield, that "In order to give a scientifically accurate definition of meaning for every form of a language, we should have to have a scientifically accurate knowledge of everything in the speakers' world," makes it clear that once a semantic theory begins to take either linguistic or nonlinguistic settings into account Pandora's box is wide open. Moreover, any effort to force its lid down again by attempting to establish significant correlations between utterances and the situations or contexts in which we use them is doomed to failure by the fact of linguistic creativity. As Katz has pointed out in an as yet unpublished monograph:

> . . . in general, the use of a natural language is free from the control of external stimuli in the speech-situation. The presence of such stimuli do [sic] not tend to increase the probability that a speaker in the situation will utter a given sentence, for . . . in typical cases, the sentence he utters will be new, and hence have a zero probability. It is, in fact, just this aspect of freedom from stimulus control that makes natural languages suitable as means for expressing the products of free thought.[35]

It seems wiser then to ignore settings altogether—at least until an adequate theory of how we interpret sentences in isolation has been formulated. This is not because the contribution that settings make to our linguistic performance is an unimportant one, but simply because we must first have a theory of linguistic competence if we are ever to have an adequate theory of performance.

Thus Katz and Fodor argue that although "Previous conceptions of semantics have usually defined the goals of a semantic description of a natural language in such a way that to achieve them a semantic theory would have to account for the manner in which settings determine how an utterance is understood . . . to

[35] *The Underlying Reality of Language and Its Philosophical Import,* xeroxed monograph, p. 62. See also Chomsky's review of B. F. Skinner's *Verbal Behavior,* in *Language,* XXXV (1959), 26–58, reprinted in *The Structure of Language,* pp. 547–578.

set the goals of a semantic theory this high is to set them too high" ("Structure of a Semantic Theory," *p. 176*). In semantics as in phonology and syntax, because the linguist is interested in competence rather than performance he is interested only in "aspects of linguistic ability which are invariant from individual to individual" *(p. 174)*. And in his monograph Katz states that in semantics this ability is the ability to recognize

> . . . the cognitive content of linguistic constructions as opposed to associated images, emotive overtones, attitudes, recollections, connotations, and metaphorical collations. Accordingly, the images and emotions evoked by the word "mother," the attitudes associated with the word "fascism," the recollections elicited by the word "childhood," the connotations of majesty and strength suggested by "lion," and the metaphorical collation found in an independent literal translation of the components of the German word "Zeitlupe" fall outside the recognized meanings of these words.[36] [*"Underlying Reality," p. 66*]

Again, it is not that these other things are uninteresting, or that we ever do use a word without associations and attitudes of some sort, but simply that they are beyond the linguist's range when he studies semantics, just as the acoustical factors that make one person's voice quality different from another's are beyond his range when he studies phonology.

The outgrowth of further work on semantics and its relations to other branches of linguistic study has been a tripartite form of linguistic description containing a syntactic component, a semantic component, and a phonological component. We need not be concerned here with the precise relations among these three components or with what specific claims the adoption of this form of linguistic description makes about the ways in which the various kinds of lin-

---

[36] Such a literal translation would be "time-magnifying-glass," but the word *"Zeitlupe"* actually means "slow motion."

guistic knowledge interact in the production and understanding of sentences.[37] Since our interest lies in seeing how linguists who share Chomsky's views conceive of meanings, we need only be concerned with the internal structure of the semantic component.

In their essay Katz and Fodor specify that the semantic component is to be composed of two sub-components, a *dictionary* and a set of what they call *projection rules*. Normally, a *dictionary entry* for a given lexical item will contain a *reading* for each of its senses. Each reading will in turn contain one or more *syntactic markers;* one or more *semantic markers;* optionally, a *distinguisher;* and, finally, a *selection restriction*. Semantic markers are enclosed in parentheses, distinguishers in brackets, and selection restrictions in angles. Thus, for example, one reading in the dictionary entry for the lexical item "honest" would be:

honest → **Adjective** → **(Evaluative)** → **(Moral)** → **[Innocent of illicit sexual intercourse]** <**(Human) and (Female)**>.

The syntactic marker merely indicates "part of speech"; the semantic markers express the general semantic properties of this sense of "honest"; the distinguisher represents what is special about this sense and thus what distinguishes it from the others; and the selection restriction tells us that in this special sense the word may only be applied to women. The projection rules contain the information required for understanding the meanings of a sentence and of its compound constituents once we know the meanings of its words. For example, when we understand the sentence "The baby is playing with a colorful ball,"

[37] For details see Jerrold J. Katz and Paul M. Postal, *An Integrated Theory of Linguistic Descriptions* (Cambridge, Mass.: M.I.T. Press, 1964), pp. 1–5 *et passim*; Chomsky, *Aspects of the Theory of Syntax*, pp. 15–18 *et passim*; and P. H. Matthews' review of *Aspects*, in *Journal of Linguistics*, III (1967), 119–152.

a rule—too complicated to quote here in its general form—would operate upon the words "colorful" and "ball" which would force us to amalgamate the reading:

colorful → **Adjective** → **(Color)** → **[Abounding in contrast or variety of bright colors]** $<$**(Physical Object) ∨ (Social Activity)**$>$.

and the reading:

ball → **Noun** → **(Physical Object)** → **(Globular Shape)**.

to produce the derived reading:

colorful + *ball* → **(Physical Object)** → **(Globular Shape)** → **(Color)** → **[Abounding in contrast or variety of bright colors]**.

This same rule, correspondingly, would prevent us from amalgamating (for example) this sense of "ball" with the sense of "colorful" represented by the reading:

colorful → **Adjective** → **(Evaluative)** → **[Having distinctive character, vividness, or picturesqueness]** $<$**(Aesthetic Object) ∨ (Social Activity)**$>$.[38]

[38] I have taken my examples of a dictionary entry and a projection rule from Katz and Postal, *An Integrated Theory of Linguistic Descriptions,* pp. 16 and 20–22. Since 1964 there have naturally been a number of new developments in semantic theory, but these need not concern us since we are only interested in getting a general idea of the *type* of theory originally proposed by Katz and Fodor. For these developments see Katz, "Recent Issues in Semantic Theory," *Foundations of Language,* III (1967), 124–194, and "Interpretative Semantics vs. Generative Semantics," *Foundations of Language,* VI (1970), 220–259. For criticisms see Uriel Weinreich, "Explorations in Semantic Theory," in Thomas A. Sebeok (ed.), *Current Trends in Linguistics,* Vol. III, *Theoretical Foundations* (The Hague: Mouton, 1966), pp. 395–477; Geoffrey N. Leech, *Towards a Semantic Description of English* (London: Longmans, 1969), Chapters I and V; Manfred Bierwisch, "On Certain Problems of Semantic

Now it seems curiously unilluminating (and perhaps a trifle disappointing) to be told that "ball" means a physical object of globular shape and that "honest" is an evaluative moral adjective. But here we should recall what Chomsky wrote at the end of one early article:

Notice that I am not saying anything new or startling when I point out that *the child seems sleeping* is not a sentence, or that *at the clown* is not a prepositional phrase in the sentence *All the children laughed at the clown.* In fact, if this information were startling, it would probably be incorrect. The linguistic study of syntactic pattern does not attempt to show that sentences are not what we think they are. Its goal is rather to explain why sentences are what we intuitively know them to be; that is, to give a kind of rational reconstruction of this intuitive knowledge.[39]

Similarly, the linguistic study of semantics does not attempt to show that words and sentences do not mean what we think they mean, but rather to explain why they mean what we intuitively know them to mean. Therefore whatever scientific value a semantic theory of the sort proposed by Katz and Fodor possesses will reside not in its ability to furnish surprising new bits of information but rather in its ability to systematize our conceptual knowledge and relate it to our other linguistic knowledge in the simplest and most revealing way possible.

Without going further into the intricacies of this sort of semantic theory, we may now ask our second question: How do linguists who share Chomsky's views conceive of meanings? To me—and again I must emphasize that I speak as an outsider and a layman—it seems that Katz's answers to this question have got

---

Representations," *Foundations of Language,* V (1969), 153–184, and "Semantics," in John Lyons (ed.), *New Horizons in Linguistics* (Harmondsworth, Middlesex: Penguin Books, 1970), pp. 166–184; and Hilary Putnam, "Is Semantics Possible?," *Metaphilosophy,* I (1970), 187–201.

[39] "Logical Structures in Language," *American Documentation,* VIII (1957), 290.

progressively clearer and more satisfying. In his essay "Semantic Theory and the Meaning of 'Good'" he says that "the semantic rules must include a *dictionary* in which each word of the language is associated with a representation of its meaning," and he speaks of meanings as being "constituted of semantic elements in relation to one another" *(p. 742)*. In *The Philosophy of Language* he says that since meanings are "composed of concepts in certain relations to one another, the job of the dictionary is to represent the conceptual structure in the meanings of words" *(p. 154)*, and at another point he goes so far as to define meanings as "representations of classes of equivalent thoughts or ideas, which thoughts and ideas are connected with linguistic constructions in the speaker's system of internalized rules" *(p. 177)*. Finally, in "The Underlying Reality of Language and Its Philosophical Import" he writes:

The distinction between linguistic competence and linguistic performance enables us to adopt a mentalistic theory of meaning without identifying meanings with particular thoughts that come into the minds of particular people at particular times and places. Just as, at the levels of phonology and syntax, we could distinguish between an utterance and a sentence, so, here, at the level of semantics, we can distinguish between a thought and a meaning. Thoughts and utterances are performance phenomena, while meanings and sentences are conceptual abstractions relating to competence. But this distinction would be of little use were we not to understand linguistic competence as the perfect knowledge of ideal speakers, for [an] actual speaker's knowledge of the meaning of a word or expression is usually only a very imperfect facsimile of its meaning in the language. [*pp. 65–66*]

Thus it becomes clear that for Katz the meanings of words are entities, but they are *abstract* entities or theoretical constructs, just as sentences are, and not concrete extralinguistic entities like physical objects or neural events. Similarly, the meanings of sentences are not situations, or features of situations, in which the sentences are used, but are also abstract conceptual entities, *compositional functions* (as Katz sometimes calls them) of the antecedently known meanings of their words.

So while this theory sounds as though it were headed for the difficulties of theories like Korzybski's and Locke's, it is not. In fact, it seems to me that this view of meanings is in some ways close to the view on which my criticism of Korzybski was implicitly based, the ordinary language philosophers' view of meanings as the roles that the rules of language allow words (or their senses) to play in normal intelligible speech. As we saw, in "The Theory of Meaning" Ryle speaks of language as "compact of rules," and in another essay, "Ordinary Language," using the analogy with chess which Wittgenstein made famous, he writes:

If I know the meaning of a word or phrase I know something like a body of unwritten rules, or something like an unwritten code or general recipe. I have learned to use the word correctly in an unlimited variety of different settings. What I know is, in this respect, somewhat like what I know when I know how to use a knight or a pawn at chess.[40]

I think that the syntactic markers, semantic markers, distinguishers, and selection restrictions that comprise Katz and Fodor's dictionary entries can be thought of as specifying what may (or may not) be done syntactically and conceptually with the word or sense in question, and thus that a dictionary entry, as they conceive it, may be thought of as an attempt to write at least some of those "unwritten rules" to which Ryle refers. Therefore it seems to me that the sort of abstract entities they have in mind when they speak of meanings are something like the rule-determined roles that ordinary language philosophers have in mind.

Yet I must add immediately that Katz takes strong exception to this comparison. The theory of meaning

[40] *The Philosophical Review,* LXII (1953), 179.

We are talking about the spatial and temporal phenomenon of language, not about some non-spatial, non-temporal phantasm. . . . But we talk about it [i.e., language] as we do about the pieces in chess when we are stating the rules of the game, not describing their physical properties.

The question "What is a word really?" is analogous to "What is a piece in chess?"[42]

And in *The Blue Book* he gives the analogy a characteristic whimsical twist: "I want to play chess, and a man gives the white king a paper crown, leaving the use of the piece unaltered, but telling me that the crown has a meaning to him in the game, which he can't express by rules. I say: 'as long as it doesn't alter the use of the piece, it hasn't what I call a meaning.' "[43]

Moreover, it seems to me that passages like these, in which Wittgenstein is using notions like *use* and *role* and *rule* to point (as it were) inward to a more or less self-contained system of linguistic or conceptual knowledge or abilities rather than outward to visible public behavior, have had a considerable influence on his followers. As we saw, Ryle says that "To know what an expression means involves knowing what can (logically) be said with it and what cannot (logically) be said with it." And Stuart Hampshire, in the essay I quoted from earlier, "The Interpretation of Language: Words and Concepts," writes:

To understand an expression in common use involves being able to recognize the standard occasions of its use, and the normal way to explain its meaning is to give specimens of these standard occasions. For every element of the vocabulary of a language which we understand, we could describe some conditions which would be the ideal conditions for the application of the expression in question; we could also describe some contrasting conditions in which its application would have to be qualified as dubious and uncertain. *[p. 274]*

[42] (Oxford: Blackwell, 1953), I, 108, p. 47e.
[43] *The Blue and Brown Books* (Oxford: Blackwell, 1958), p. 65.

We can also find similar passages in the two essays that contain perhaps the two most famous defenses of ordinary language philosophy, Gilbert Ryle's "Ordinary Language" and J. L. Austin's 'A Plea For Excuses."[44] Ryle begins by pointing out that as he is using the word, "ordinary" means "standard" or "stock" rather than "common" or "current" or "colloquial" *(pp. 167–171)*. Later he refers to his sort of philosophizing as "the extraction of the logical rules implicitly governing a concept" *(p. 177)* and speaks of himself and his colleagues as "interested in the informal logic of the employment of expressions" *(p. 186)*. And Austin insists that in conducting philosophical analysis "we are dealing with *imagined* situations" *(p. 48)*.

From such passages it seems to me clear that a good deal of the time at least, ordinary language philosophers are as interested in an idealization—standard or normal English—and in what Katz called "the perfect knowledge of ideal speakers" as are Chomskyan linguists. Thus despite some of the implications of the phrase "ordinary language," the philosophers, like the linguists, are not concerned with mere verbal behavior, or with "the public aspects of the ways speakers use words and sentences in social intercourse," as ends in themselves but rather as evidence, for what light they can shed on this idealization. One can find other passages in their work that contradict this conclusion, but one can also find many that confirm it; and I must confess that if words like "standard," "ideal," and "logically" are not being used in the passages quoted above to appeal to such an idealization, I do not see how they are being used.

If I am right in thinking there are important similarities between the ways ordinary language philosophers and Chomskyan linguists conceive of meanings, then the fact from which we began, the fact that the

[44] *Philosophical Papers*, J. O. Urmson and G. J. Warnock (eds.) (Oxford: Oxford University Press, 1961), pp. 123–152.

philosophers have not developed any general notion of linguistic structure, seems all the stranger. For as we saw, Chomsky's notion of structure resulted from his conviction that the linguist studies an idealization that abstracts away from the linguistically irrelevant aspects of utterances, and it was this idea that led Katz and Fodor to approach semantics as they did. Katz's criticism of the philosophers for failing to develop such a notion would then seem all the more justified, as would related criticisms that have recently been advanced against them—that they never fully specify the rules for using a given expression and that they never specify generally and precisely just what a rule of language is. Whether such criticisms are in fact justified or whether Hampshire is right in saying that "the interest of contemporary philosophers in forms of speech neither is, nor should be, scientific or systematic," is an issue I cannot hope to settle. For my own part, I am not at all sure what the sort of analysis practiced by ordinary language philosophers would gain from having behind it a general conception of linguistic structure of the sort proposed by Chomsky (or of any other sort, for that matter). Speaking of meanings as a matter of rules and roles seems to me to have more a negative than a positive value for the philosophers: it prevents them from making the philosophical mistakes that resulted from thinking of meanings as some sort of real entities.

Moreover, the ordinary language philosophers' concern with meaning seems different in character from that of the linguists; some of the differences emerge quite clearly in a recent, and rather well-known, disagreement among three of the philosophers. In *The Concept of Mind* Ryle sought to clear up some problems about the will by contrasting the ordinary use of the terms "voluntary" and "involuntary" with what he claimed was a special, and misleadingly extended, philosophical use of them. In the course of this analysis he wrote:

In their most ordinary employment "voluntary" and "involuntary" are used, with a few minor elasticities, as adjectives applying to actions which ought not to be done. We discuss whether someone's action was voluntary or not only when the action seems to have been his fault. . . .

In this ordinary use, then, it is absurd to discuss whether satisfactory, correct or admirable performances are voluntary or involuntary. . . .

But philosophers, in discussing what constitutes acts voluntary or involuntary, tend to describe as voluntary not only reprehensible but also meritorious actions, not only things that are someone's fault but also things that are to his credit.[45]

Now Austin, in a quite different connection, had remarked in "A Plea For Excuses" that "we may join the army or make a gift voluntarily" (p. 58). And Stanley Cavell, another ordinary language philosopher,[46] noting that "There is clearly a clash here," since "making a gift is not always something which ought not to be done, or something which is always someone's fault," offered a qualification of Ryle's point:

Although we can (sometimes) say, "The gift was made voluntarily," it is specifically not something we can say about ordinary, unremarkable cases of making gifts. Only when the action (or circumstances) of making the gift is in some way unusual (instead of his usual Christmas bottle, you give the neighborhood policeman a check for $1000), or extraordinary (you leave your heirs penniless and bequeath your house to your cat), or untoward (you give your rocking horse to your new friend, but the next morning you cry to have it back), can the question whether it was voluntary intelligibly arise. . . .

Not seeing that the condition for applying the term "voluntary" holds quite generally—viz., the condition that there be something (real or imagined) fishy about any performance intelligibly so characterized—Ryle construes the condition too narrowly, supposes that there must be something morally fishy about the performance. [pp. 174, 176–177]

[45] (London: Hutchinson, 1949), p. 69.

[46] "Must We Mean What We Say?," Inquiry, I (1958), 172–212. See also Katz and Fodor's reply, "The Availability of What We Say," The Philosophical Review, LXXII (1963), 57–71.

Now the point is not whether Cavell's solution of the "clash" between Ryle and Austin is right or not, or even whether this sort of linguistic analysis is philosophically illuminating or not. The point is rather that the philosophers are investigating meaning differently from the way Katz says the linguist should investigate it. They too are trying to reconstruct an ideal speaker's linguistic intuitions under certain imagined circumstances rather than simply describing any particular real speakers and circumstances, but they are plainly going beyond the bare "cognitive content" that Katz said the linguist working in semantics should restrict himself to. This seems clear, whether we call the hint of "fishiness" (moral or otherwise) allegedly attaching to "voluntary" one of those "associations" or "overtones" that Katz said were no business of the linguist or merely call it a further implication of the word's conceptual relations—and it doesn't really seem to matter which we call it. Moreover, the philosophers are not considering sentences in isolation but are imagining particular linguistic and nonlinguistic contexts[47] in attempting to determine the rules or conditions for correctly applying or withholding the term "voluntary."

Therefore it is not just that ordinary language philosophers are, as Hampshire's comment implies, interested only in special parts of the language rather than in all of it, as a linguist is; it is also that in investigating meaning they are interested in making

---

[47] Their tendency to do this has increased with the recent concentration of attention on speech acts. The investigation of speech acts was initiated by Austin in certain of his *Philosophical Papers*, advanced by him in his posthumously published book *How to Do Things with Words*, J. O. Urmson (ed.) (Cambridge, Mass.: Harvard University Press, 1962), and is now carried on by Searle and others. "The total speech act in the total speech situation," Austin wrote in *How to Do Things with Words*, "is the *only actual* phenomenon which, in the last resort, we are engaged in elucidating" (p. 147). See also K. T. Fann (ed.), *Symposium on J. L. Austin* (New York: Humanities Press, 1969).

a deeper cut (so to speak) than a linguist is. The linguistic intuitions they seek to reconstruct are not necessarily "invariant" among all speakers of the language but are quite special, and the situations they imagine are fleshed out to the point where the rules they are talking about do come close to being regulative (rather than constitutive) rules—if not exactly like the rules of etiquette, then perhaps something like the rules of verbal etiquette which we find in books like Fowler's *Modern English Usage*. In any case, they are demanding a greater degree of verbal sensitivity from their ideal speaker than the linguists do.

That this should be so becomes understandable when we consider what the philosophers are usually trying to accomplish. Ryle's treatment of "voluntary" is characteristic of their work in that it involves bringing one ("ordinary") part of the language to bear on another ("philosophical") part in order to reveal something odd or misleading about the latter. Like Katz and Fodor, they too are interested in semantic anomalies, but the ones that interest them do not result from large crude category mistakes of the sort that produce sentences like "The paint is silent," but are far more subtle—indeed, if they were not, they would not need analyzing. If someone failed to see that there was something odd about "The paint is silent" we should be justified in saying he did not know English—and of course the reason that Katz and Fodor are interested only in such large mistakes is that a speaker's knowledge of English is what they are interested in characterizing. But the anomalies the philosophers are interested in have been produced and tolerated by speakers who are not merely fluent but are very intelligent and sophisticated as well: philosophers. Moreover, it is often the case that they have been produced and tolerated only by such speakers and not by less sophisticated ones, for even to make the mistakes that result in such anomalies

SEMANTICS, LINGUISTICS, AND CRITICISM

involves having certain questions arise that do not arise ordinarily but only in the course of thinking philosophically. (Yet it should perhaps be added that there is something peculiarly tempting about these mistakes and that most ordinary people will be led to make them once they start trying to think philosophically.)

We have seen that the sort of semantic theory proposed by Katz and Fodor is more promising as a scientific study of meaning than general semantics proved to be; and our examination of Chomsky's conception of linguistics, and of the place that semantics occupies within that conception, has perhaps suggested some of the reasons why it is more promising. But in conclusion I would also suggest that our acceptance of this sort of semantic theory does not at all commit us to agreeing with Katz's criticisms of ordinary language philosophy. In *The Philosophy of Language* he complains about the "thoroughgoing distrust of generalizations" that underlies "the ordinary language philosopher's avoidance of any systematic or theoretical concern with language and his corresponding preoccupation with only the most minute details of English," and to this distrust he contrasts "the scientific view that explanation consists in the systematization of detailed facts in the form of generalizations that reveal their underlying organization" *(p. 90)*. The assumption behind his criticisms of ordinary language philosophy is thus that explanations in all fields of inquiry aim at the generality admittedly aimed at by scientific explanations. All explanations are therefore precise or adequate or useful just to the extent that they are general. As we turn in the next chapter to the question towards which we have been heading all along, the question of whether or not the scientific study of meaning can be of any help to the reader or critic of literature, we shall have ample opportunity to see the confusions that can result from this assumption.

semantics
and
criticism

Though in the last fifteen years or so there has been a steady increase in the number of attempts to demonstrate the usefulness of linguistics to the reader or critic of literature, none of them, so far as I know, has dealt specifically with semantics. In fact the critical usefulness of semantics, as opposed to phonology and syntax, has sometimes been explicitly denied. For example Harold Whitehall, after remarking that "as no science can go beyond mathematics, no criticism can go beyond its linguistics," adds:

And the kind of linguistics needed by recent criticism for the solution of its pressing problems of metrics and stylistics, in fact, for all problems of the linguistic surface of letters, is not semantics, either epistemological or communicative, but down-to-the-surface linguistics, microlinguistics not metalinguistics.[1]

But of course Whitehall is writing from a pre-Chomskyan point of view, and when he speaks of semantics he is thinking of the nebulous, unproductive sort of semantics we saw in Bloomfield and his followers, or perhaps of I. A. Richards' early efforts to establish a science of criticism within a larger science of symbolism. Just as the recent enrichment of syntactic theory that has come with the advent of transformational grammar has produced a number of attempts to demonstrate the relevance of syntax to criticism, so it seems likely that the work of Katz and Fodor reviewed in the preceding chapter will soon lead linguists interested in literature to turn their attention to semantics. I have heard this suggested more than once in conversation, and Richard Ohmann, the most interesting and articulate supporter of the critical relevance of transformational syntactic theory, has remarked that "It is no surprise . . . to find stylistics in a state of disorganization when syntax and semantics, upon which stylistics clearly depends, have themselves been hampered by the lack of a theory that is inclusive, unified, and plausible."[2]

As I said in my Introduction, I cannot see that any of these attempts, whether carried on within the framework of phonology or of syntax, have yielded anything significant, and I do not think that future attempts, whether involving semantics or not, will have any better success. Yet I think the subject is very much worth pursuing because I think the reasons for their failure are very interesting ones. I do not, that is, take the position so often taken by people trained in literature who write about these matters: that

[1] "From Linguistics to Criticism," *The Kenyon Review*, XVIII (1956), 415.

[2] "Generative Grammars and the Concept of Literary Style," *Word*, XX (1964), 425.

linguists, by virtue of being (or at least claiming to be) scientists, are thereby insensitive and unfit to deal with poetry. It is true that a number of the linguists have written very crudely and mechanically about poetry and its workings, but Ohmann is an extremely sensitive reader of literature, and what I take to be the failure of his attempts to establish the critical relevance of transformational syntactic theory has nothing whatever to do with a lack of critical qualifications. Rather, the failure of his and other attempts to make linguistics relevant to criticism seems to me to depend on an important mistake about the nature of critical explanation and about the logic of a certain central group of concepts operative in criticism. In trying to show why I think that any future attempts involving semantics are also doomed to failure, I shall first review what I hope is a fair and representative sampling of the work already done with phonology and syntax; then, since the mistake I refer to emerges still more clearly in the early work of I. A. Richards, I shall try to show the form it takes there; finally I shall try to correct the mistake.

I

I think it is fair to say that all the writers who are interested in applying linguistics to criticism share two large general assumptions. The first of these is that criticism, as it now stands, is unsatisfactory because it is impressionistic and subjective. Archibald Hill speaks of the tendency of some students of literature, influenced by critics like Matthew Arnold, "to believe that unchecked subjectivity is a legitimate method of analysis";[3] and Garland Cannon refers approvingly to Hill's rejection of "Arnold's touchstone method

[3] "A Program for the Definition of Literature," *Texas Studies in English*, XXXVII (1958), 47.

and all such impressionistic inquiry."[4] Seymour Chatman more modestly voices the hope that while the "simple, descriptive tasks" that linguistics can perform cannot "help the critic to a judgment or the historian to an account," they may nonetheless "help us to document our judgments or illustrate our facts and, in so doing, relieve us of some of our impressionistic urges."[5] Michael Riffaterre asserts that "Subjective impressionism, normative rhetoric and premature aesthetic evaluation have long interfered with the development of stylistics as a science, especially as a science of literary styles."[6] It would not be hard to extend the list.

The second assumption (predictably enough) is that if the critic is to make his impressionistic remarks clear and objective, he needs the help of the linguist. "It is quite clear," writes Edward Stankiewicz, "that the study of verbal art is intimately connected with, and must be based on, the study of language—the linguist's discipline";[7] and Roman Jakobson goes so far as to assert that since "Poetics deals with problems of verbal structure" and "linguistics is the global science of verbal structure," therefore "poetics may be regarded as an integral part of linguistics."[8] Again the list could easily be extended, but it is more to the point to see what lies behind this second assumption.

Archibald Hill prefaces an analysis[9] of Gerard Manley Hopkins' poem "The Windhover" thus:

[4] "Linguistics and Literature," *College English,* XXI (1960), 255.

[5] "Linguistics, Poetics, and Interpretation: the Phonemic Dimension," *The Quarterly Journal of Speech,* XLIII (1957), 248.

[6] "Criteria for Style Analysis," *Word,* XV (1959), 154.

[7] "Linguistics and the Study of Poetic Language," in Thomas A. Sebeok (ed.), *Style in Language* (New York: Technology Press of M.I.T. and John Wiley, 1960), p. 69.

[8] "From the Viewpoint of Linguistics: Closing Statement: Linguistics and Poetics," in *Style in Language,* p. 350.

[9] "An Analysis of *The Windhover:* An Experiment in Structural Method," *PMLA,* LXX (1955), 968–978.

The analysis is based on a number of assumptions. It is assumed that a poem, like a painting or a molecule, has structure. That is, the parts occur in such a fashion that their relation can be described, and used for prediction of recurrence. It follows that the analyst does his best to discover this structure, and to make a statement of it. . . .

Secondly, poems are a sub-class of utterances, included within the larger class of all instances of language use. It follows from this that it ought, at least ideally, to be worthwhile to turn to the science of linguistics to see if this activity, which has as its goal the systematic analysis of language and language use, has anything to contribute, in method or results, to the analysis of poetry. [pp. 968–969]

And Sol Saporta writes that while "The linguist cannot study poetry as art without abandoning his position as linguist," nevertheless "it may turn out that the analysis of poetry as language will in some way correlate with, or be a complement to, the analysis of the same phenomena as art, at the same time utilizing more precise techniques."[10] Saporta continues:

Underlying any linguistic analysis of poetry is the hypothesis that there will be some significant correlation with the results of other, more intuitive methods. The results must in some way coincide with our intuitions about the nature of the phenomena, or we are obliged to doubt their validity. When our analysis does not coincide with our intuitions, usually we find it necessary to modify our analysis; only rarely do we find it necessary to modify our intuitions. Terms like *value*, *aesthetic purpose*, etc., are apparently an essential part of the methods of most literary criticism, but such terms are not available to linguists. The statements that linguists make will include references to phonemes, stresses, morphemes, syntactical patterns, etc., and their patterned repetition and co-occurrence. It remains to be demonstrated to what extent an analysis of messages based on such features will correlate with that made in terms of value and purpose. [p. 83]

What Hill and Saporta are saying quite explicitly,

[10] "The Application of Linguistics to the Study of Poetic Language," in *Style in Language*, p. 83.

and what the other linguists I have cited are implying, is that a literary critic's analysis of a poetic text and a linguist's analysis of it are going in the same direction. In addition, most of the other linguists also assume that the linguist's analysis goes further than the critic's and is thus in some way a completion of it. This is why they think that if the critic is to attain objectivity and escape the censure of impressionism, he must let the linguist clarify his analysis for him.

Now it is important to note that while these writers repeatedly maintain that the critic's concern with value is what especially opens him to charges of impressionism and subjectivity, ordinary value-judgments—i.e., statements containing in their predicates out-and-out value-words like "good," "bad," "excellent," and so on—are not the statements that they think are most in need of clarification. As the passages I have quoted suggest, the statements they are really interested in are rather the kind that we often use to explain or support a value-judgment, statements that contain in their predicates words like "pattern," "design," "unity," and "structure." They are interested, that is, in discovering the underlying linguistic pattern or structure that the critic is really (though unclearly) talking about when he uses these vague intuitive words and lets it go at that.

Most of their attempts to do this have been carried out in terms of phonemes, either ordinary segmental phonemes or the so-called suprasegmental phonemes such as stress, juncture, and intonation. A good example of the former sort of analysis is James J. Lynch's essay "The Tonality of Lyric Poetry: An Experiment in Method,"[11] which attempts to show a significant relation between phonemic patterning and meaning in a number of short poems. In Keats's "On First Looking into Chapman's Homer," the poem

[11] *Word*, IX (1953), 211–224.

Lynch treats in greatest detail, he concludes that part of the poem's unity stems from the fact that the crucial word from the standpoint of meaning—"silent" in the final line "Silent, upon a peak in Darien"—is also composed of the sounds dominant in the rest of the poem:

The dominant phonemes, we found, are [n, d, l, t] and [s]; [aⁱ] and [ə]. One of these, [d], we saw, became much less important as the sonnet progressed so that all of its original strength is likely not to be felt by the time a reading of the sonnet is ended. Now, if we rearrange the remaining phonemes thus—[s aⁱ l ə n t] —we can see that the word we found to occupy such an important position for numerous reasons, which in fact sums up the theme of the sonnet, also sums up its dominant sound structure. The poet's "sixth sense," whether operating consciously or unconsciously, led him to consummate his poem not only in terms appropriate to his meaning, but also in terms which climax the workings of the lyrical faculty on its most basic level, sound. *[p. 219]*

And in Wordsworth's "I wandered lonely as a cloud" Lynch finds a similar relation between the most important words of the poem's climactic statement —"dances" and "daffodils" in the lines "And then my heart with pleasure fills, / And dances with the daffodils"—and its overall phonemic pattern:

. . . the dominant sounds in the poem are [l, n, d, t, s] and [z] of the consonants, and [æ, ə] and [ɪ] of the vowels. All of these are relatively stable throughout the entire poem except [t], which steadily diminishes in importance after the second stanza. On the other hand, [f], a phoneme almost invariably far down the list and here completely inoperative in stanzas two and three, supplants [t] in importance in the final stanza where it is outranked only by [l, n] and [d]. Thus, most of both the persistently dominant and the climactically dominant sound structure of the poem is caught up in the last word [d æ f ə d ɪ l z], and the rest in the other prominent word in the last line [d æ n s ə z]. *[p. 220]*

After several more such analyses he concludes:

... it seems clear even after no greater application than this (1) that choice of phonemes, especially of all the vowels and of those consonants not among the most frequent sounds of ordinary spoken English, if subjected to more extended study, may be found to support and perhaps to modify the findings of other kinds of critical analysis as to the poetic practices of individual writers, and (2) that tonally (i.e., phonemically) as well as ideationally there are *kinds* of poetic structures—which in large measure coincide. *[pp. 223–224]*

In an essay I cited earlier, "Linguistics, Poetics, and Interpretation: the Phonemic Dimension," Seymour Chatman seems to me to have put his finger on what is wrong with Lynch's analyses. After asserting that Lynch considered "statistics *in vacuo* without any real definition to give them relevance," Chatman continues:

I don't mean to suggest that statistics are wholly to be despised. But their use is paradoxical: We count features only to demonstrate that they are distinctive enough to be noticed *without* recourse to statistics; the count is significant only insofar as it corresponds to a preformed impression in the sensitive reader's mind. *[p. 250]*

Despite Lynch's reassurance that his method of analysis "was constructed only after the qualities which it demonstrates objectively were vaguely suspected as present" *("Tonality of Lyric Poetry," p. 212)*, I think the facts he points out about the key words of the Keats and Wordsworth poems are critically irrelevant precisely because I don't see how it could possibly be established (or even reasonably claimed) that such facts ought to enter into and contribute to that "sensitive reader's" total response to the poems. You might of course be aware of them while responding to the poems—as you might also be aware that Keats's poem was composed on a given day of the week or that Wordsworth's contained a certain number of commas—but that is quite a different matter. At the very least, some argument would be required to establish their critical relevance.

The same sort of objection could be advanced against most of the positive points made in essays like Lynch's—against, for example, David I. Masson's fanciful contention that one source of the effectiveness of Keats's line "No hungry generations tread thee down" is "the rising-and-sinking (or, taking into account the lowest formants of the vowels, more correctly *expanding-and-contracting*) pattern nuá i é éi é áun."[12] Some years ago Dell Hymes, in a paper called "Phonological Aspects of Style: Some English Sonnets,"[13] pretty much closed the case for this sort of phonemic analysis of poetry. Hymes applied Lynch's methods to an extent (and with results) that led another linguist present at the same conference to comment: "We should be grateful because he has carried out this laborious method of phoneme counting and phoneme weighting on a big enough corpus so that we can now say fairly confidently that (in this form at any rate) it is a waste of time. [Laughter.]"[14] Moreover, in the course of his analysis Hymes made a point very similar to Chatman's:

> Another limitation which, as far as I know, all stylistic approaches share is the making of untested assumptions about the psychology of poet or audience. Many of these assumptions are reasonable and intuitively correct to the student or practitioner of verbal art. But we do not in fact know that the use of a sound in one part of a poem has any effect on a reader in a subsequent part; we have no "just noticeable differences" for the prominence of sounds by repetition in a sonnet. Rather, we analyze the poem, construct an interpretation, and postulate (or instruct) the reader's response. *[p. 130]*

Thus in recent years linguists interested in the appli-

[12] "Vowel and Consonant Patterns in Poetry," *The Journal of Aesthetics and Art Criticism,* XII (1953), 217.

[13] In *Style in Language,* pp. 109–131.

[14] Fred W. Householder, Jr., "From the Viewpoint of Linguistics: Opening Statement," in *Style in Language,* p. 343.

cation of phonology to criticism have tended to shift their attention from segmental to suprasegmental phonemes, especially to the ways in which knowledge of the suprasegmental system of English can help to solve problems of metrics. In fact Chatman criticized Lynch precisely in order to make the point that "The literary implications of *supra*segmental phonemics— the system of stress and intonation features in language—are much more exciting" *(p. 252)* than those of segmental phonemics.

To justify this assertion Chatman produces four examples of "occasions when the linguist's ears may catch a significant item, one which tells us something about what happens between the printed page and the interpreter's lips" *(p. 253)*. First he takes Claudius' lines from *Hamlet* (III, i, 60–61): "'. . . but 'tis not so above; / There is no shuffling." Employing the system of notation introduced by George L. Trager and Henry Lee Smith in *An Outline of English Structure*,[15] Chatman writes:

Contrast these interpretations: ²*There is no* ³*shuffling* and ³*Thére*² | ²*is no* ³*shuffling*¹#. In the first interpretation, a tertiary stress is used on *is* to fill the metrical point (that is, the "iamb" is observed), turning *there* into a mere expletive: "No shuffling exists." In the second interpretation, *there* is "promoted," a stress shift occurs, and *there* is correctly interpreted as a spatial adverb: "No shuffling can be found in that place." *[p. 253]*

His second example is from Donne's "Twickenham Garden" (lines 19–21):

[15] (Norman, Okla.: Battenburg Press, 1951), pp. 35–52. Unlike the symbols used to represent segmental phonemes in the passages just quoted from Lynch's essay, the Trager-Smith notation demands some explanation. Primary (i.e., strongest) stresses are represented by ´, secondary by ˆ, and tertiary by ˋ; levels of pitch, going from low to high, are represented by the superscript numbers ¹, ², and ³ respectively; and degree of juncture, ranging from a slight pause to a sentence-break, are represented by |, ||, and # respectively.

> Hither with crystal vials, lovers come
> And take my tears, which are love's wine,
> And try your mistress' tears at home.

Because many editions of the poem fail to place a comma after "lovers," Chatman first read the opening line as though it meant "Lovers are coming with crystal vials," thus: ²*Hîther wìth crŷstal ³víals²* | ³*lóvers côme²* | ²*And tâke mỳ ³téars¹* #. But now, he tells us, the sense of the third line has led him to construe "lovers" as a vocative and "take" as an imperative, so that sense becomes "Please come, lovers, with crystal vials," and the line is rendered thus in the Trager-Smith notation: ²*Hîther wìth crŷstal³ vials²* | ²*lóvers* || ³*cóme¹* #. Chatman then asserts:

> This example clearly demonstrates the incapacity of convential metrics to show significant meaning contrasts. The conventional marking would be simply to put stress marks over *lov-* and *come*, and to leave it at that—but leaving it at that leaves it totally ambiguous. Naturally both syllables are stressed. The question is to what degree? *[p. 254]*

For his third example he cites these lines from *The Faerie Queene* (I, ii, 13): "And like a Persian mitre on her hed / Shee wore, with crowns and owches garnished." He then comments:

> One must resist the temptation to read *And lîke a Pêrsian mítre.* The obvious meaning, "Like a Persian, she wore a mitre on her head," requires something more like the following: *And lìke a ³Pérsian¹* # ³*mítre¹* | ¹*on her³héd ²Sheè wôre.* *[p. 254]*

Finally he calls attention to the word "above" in Shelley's line "The sphere-fire above its soft colors wove" ("The Cloud," line 70) in order to show that "Sometimes stress and juncture provide the only way in which one can distinguish between parts of speech capable of class-cleavage":

> Is *above* a preposition ("The sphere-fire wove above its soft colors") or an adverb ("The sphere-fire, above, wove its soft colors")? The context obviously requires the adverbial interpretation; so we must read something like: *The ²sphère-fìre a³bóve || ²its sòft ³cólors² | ²wove¹#*. (It would probably be a mistake to read *The ³sphére-²fìre | ²abòve its sôft ³cólors | ²wóve¹#*.) *[p. 254]*

The difficulty here seems to me precisely opposite to the difficulty with Lynch's essay: here phonemic analysis is not being used to turn up facts that are critically irrelevant; rather, the critically relevant (and indeed elementary) facts are ascertained in a way that has nothing whatever to do with either phonemic analysis or the Trager-Smith notation. In a published letter of reply to Chatman's essay[16] John C. McLaughlin pointed out that "nothing in the world but the syntax is going to tell us that 'Persian' . . . is a substantive and not a modifier" in the Spenser example, that the same is true of "above" in the Shelley example, and that the reading Chatman recommends for the Donne example "is the only reading of the line syntactically possible" (p. 177). In fact Chatman's own way of putting it makes clear that the deciding factor in every case was "context," and hence that the decision between interpretations could have been made without any knowledge of suprasegmental phonemics and without employing (or even being able to decipher) the Trager-Smith notation or any other like it.

Chatman does say in conclusion that what he has shown "is perfectly apparent to readers who understand poetry, and it tells us nothing new and wonderful about the poems," and he describes his purpose as

[16] *The Quarterly Journal of Speech,* XLIV (1958), 175–178.

being "simply to show that linguists have developed a graphic system which can help us talk about such things in a clearer and more consistent way than before" *(p. 254)*. But what gain in clarity or consistency is actually achieved by the use of the Trager-Smith notation? What we are faced with initially in each case is a pair of alternative interpretations of a line or two of poetry, and hence it is these interpretations, as well as the grounds for choosing one of them over the other, that we are trying to "talk about." But the notation does not give us a means of talking about these interpretations at all, let alone of doing so "in a clearer and more consistent way than before," for all it provides in each case is a means of notating graphically the normal realization in sound of each interpretation. By initially presenting us, in all but the Shelley example, not with two normally written English paraphrases of the two possible interpretations of the lines in question but rather with two transcriptions in the Trager-Smith notation— which he actually calls "interpretations" in the case of the *Hamlet* example—Chatman obscures this fact and makes it look as though the choice were between the two transcriptions (or the two sequences of sounds they transcribe) and as though the notation itself had somehow functioned as a heuristic device. Certainly there are many occasions on which "the linguist's ears may catch" something the ears of the rest of us don't catch, but that special ability can only be of help to us when we are trying to distinguish between alternative sequences of sounds (as, for example, when we are trying to tell from his accent which of two Texans comes from Houston), not (as here) when we are trying to decide between alternative interpretations of sense.

Another difficulty with Chatman's sort of metrical analysis is that it tends to deflect attention from the poem itself—a public linguistic or cultural object that different readers can experience, argue about, and so on—to one or more oral performances of the poem, usually on phonograph records or magnetic tape. In another essay, "Robert Frost's 'Mowing': an Inquiry into Prosodic Structure,"[17] Chatman analyzes eight different recorded performances of the poem, including Frost's own. Here too the problems that Chatman seems to claim are solved by the Trager-Smith notation are really solved by other means. For example, of the last line of the poem, "My long scythe whispered and left the hay to make," he writes:

> The word ["make"] is used in a special intransitive sense which my city-bred ears had never heard before: "dry out." On the first reading I had carelessly assumed that the subject of "make" was "scythe" and that "hay" was the inverted object (which, of course, didn't make any sense at all). Frost's performance clears up the problem by giving "hay" secondary stress and "make" primary; that is, I had read *lêft the háy to mâke*, but Frost reads *lêft the hây to máke*. This important distinction would be totally lost in any conventional notation, which would probably mark both "hay" and "make" as "stressed," and leave it at that. *[p. 431]*

Here the suggestion is not only (as before) that the solution of the problem required a knowledge of the Trager-Smith notation but that it required hearing "Frost's performance" as well. One wants to reply not only that Frost's or any other adequate performance could have solved the problem for someone not trained in suprasegmental phonemics but also (as before) that the problem could equally well have been solved without hearing anybody's performance, simply by virtue of the prior fact that the rejected interpretation "didn't make any sense."

This deflection of attention to recorded performances also creates more general problems for the linguist interested in poetry. Because critical remarks are characteristically about one poem rather than

[17] *The Kenyon Review,* XVIII (1956), 421–438.

many performances of it, it is natural that when the linguist searching for the linguistic facts that underlie and explain critical remarks finds himself faced with different performances of the same poem, he should not want to let the matter rest in sheer observed diversity but should rather want to go on to claim that one performance is better or more authoritative than the others. But how are such decisions to be made? As Garland Cannon has pointed out in the essay I cited earlier, "Linguistics and Literature," "every new reading of a work is unique from all previous readings," and "there seems to be no one authoritative reading (or reader) of a given utterance once it has become permanent" (p. 258). Chatman's Frost essay suggests that there is a natural tendency to assume that the poet's own reading will be the authoritative one, and Cannon does add the qualification that "degrees of reliability exist, in that if a linguist could secure a recording of a poet reading his work only moments after he had finished composing it, the phonemic transcription of the recording would presumably be a more desirable corpus for analysis than would a transcription of the linguist's reading of the poem" (p. 258). But of course such recordings are almost always out of the question in the case of dead poets, and even in the case of living ones they are not often available. Moreover, our knowledge of the suprasegmentals of English at other periods of history is less than adequate. Cannon is thus led to the rather pessimistic conclusion that "it would seem that linguistic analysis, both phonological and structural, should not be made of non-modern poetry except with the most cautious qualifications" (p. 259)—an admission which, if true, would severely limit the relevance of linguistics to criticism.

Still another difficulty resulting from the deflection of attention to various performances of the poem under consideration is that linguists have often been led to claim that ambiguities which cannot be preserved in oral performance are therefore not properly part of the poem at all. For example Chatman, in a short essay called "Mr. Stein on Donne,"[18] contends that an ambiguity pointed out by Arnold Stein in one of Donne's elegies "demands a resolution in oral performance" and is therefore "a paper ambiguity only," which

> . . . in terms of the sound the line will assume, is more apparent than real. The mind may persist, but the voice is required to make a choice between the alternatives by the very structure of the language. . . . The voice has no mechanism for "hovering," at least if it is to remain an English voice speaking English. . . . In this line ambiguity can only exist between the printed page and the reader's eye, not between the performer's voice and the audience's ear. But then what we have is a problem in textual interpretation, not one in metrics. *[pp. 449–450]*

This seems fair enough, but of course if we are interested in showing the relevance of linguistics to criticism, it is often "problems of textual interpretation" that we are interested in, as Chatman's choice of examples in his other two essays makes clear; and at any rate, such problems cannot simply be dismissed without greatly oversimplifying the critic's function. As Samuel R. Levin pointed out in an answer to Chatman, sometimes "ambiguity is composed into a poem" and therefore the performance relevant to the critic is "that type of performance which optimally sustains that ambiguity, . . . a visual performance, by which is meant a silent reading."[19]

As I suggested at the beginning of this chapter, it is only recently that linguists interested in criticism have turned their attention from phonology to syntax. Syntactic considerations enter Levin's short book *Lin-*

[18] *The Kenyon Review,* XVIII (1956), 443–451.

[19] "Suprasegmentals and the Performance of Poetry," *The Quarterly Journal of Speech,* XLVIII (1962), 369.

guistic Structures in Poetry, but the book as a whole is so vague and open-ended that it is hard to reach any conclusion about their potential usefulness. Levin starts by asserting that poetry's two basic characteristics are "that it is unified and that it is memorable,"[20] and he then sets out to supply a linguistic explanation for these qualities. Since "poetry consists of language, yet produces effects that ordinary language does not produce," Levin infers "that poetry is language differently ordered or arranged" *(p. 11)*. This difference he takes to lie in the fact that poetry, unlike ordinary language, employs a device which he calls *coupling,* "the structure wherein naturally equivalent forms . . . occur in equivalent positions" *(pp. 34–35)*. A few pages later he explains:

In ordinary messages, we usually find no relation existing between two forms occurring at corresponding positions in the message, beyond the fact that they both belong to the same Type I paradigm—the one defined by that position [i.e., beyond the fact that the two forms are both grammatically possible]—and that they serve to communicate what is intended. Poetic messages, as we have seen, very often do show this additional relation, however: that the forms occurring in corresponding positions are related to each other also semantically or phonically. . . . In other words, in poetry, constructions are not merely dummies, to be filled in by just any linguistic forms as long as they are grammatical and communication is effected; in poetry the constructions are filled by words having the special kinds of equivalence that we have described. *[p. 39]*

But while coupling both "serves to unify a poem" and "is what makes a poem memorable" *(p. 39)*, Levin believes that "it would be a mistake to conclude that the more couplings one finds or puts in a poem, the better is that poem," for while "the poet's task is to achieve a unity out of complex factors," this unity "must not be achieved at the expense of complexity"

[20] (The Hague: Mouton, 1962), p. 10.

(p. 48). Thus Levin concludes that the degree of coupling that is desirable will depend "on the simultaneous action and interaction of all the other factors that operate in a poem" *(p. 48)*. This of course tells us virtually nothing, and our confidence in Levin's methods is not increased when we notice that in order to find the couplings he wants to find in Shakespeare's "When to the sessions of sweet silent thought," the only poem he considers at length, he has to alter it in several ways—or as he puts it, to base his statements "on a normalization of the poem and not on the poem itself" *(p. 54)*. The most important of these alterations is the substitution for Shakespeare's last line ("All losses are restored and sorrows end") of one that is of Levin's own devising and that has a quite different meaning: "Then you restore all losses and you end sorrows."

There is a good deal more to catch hold of in Ohmann's essays. His interest in syntax has led him to attempt a general characterization of the concept of style, and this in turn has led him to try to specify the transformational machinery that gives particular writers' styles their distinctive qualities. Therefore the allegedly impressionistic critical terms that he is most interested in finding linguistic correlates or explanations for are not large general terms like "design" and "unity" but rather the metaphorical descriptive terms we apply to particular styles, terms we may perhaps think of as standing at a still further remove from ordinary value-words. He has given two illustrative lists of these terms. In "Prolegomena to the Analysis of Prose Style"[21] he writes: "the method which I suggest saves the study of style from having to rely *only* on those impressionistic, metaphorical judgments which have too often substituted for analysis: dignified, grand, plain, decorative, placid, exuberant,

[21] In Harold C. Martin (ed.), *Style in Prose Fiction*, English Institute Essays, 1958 (New York: Columbia University Press, 1959), pp. 1–24.

restrained, hard, and the whole tired assortment of epithets which name without explaining" *(p. 14)*. And in the essay I cited at the beginning of this chapter, "Generative Grammars and the Concept of Literary Style," Ohmann defines impressionism as "the application of metaphorical labels to styles ('masculine,' 'limber,' 'staccato,' 'flowing,' 'involuted,' etc.), and the attempt to evaluate (Swift's style is the best, or the most natural to English)" *(p. 424)*.

The latter essay opens with a catalogue of common methods of stylistic analysis. Ohmann then comments:

> And indeed, the inability of these and other methods, in spite of many partial successes, to yield a full and convincing explication of the notion of style seems in general to follow from the absence of an appropriate underlying linguistic and semantic theory. A style is a characteristic use of language, and it is difficult to see how the *uses* of a system can be understood unless the system itself has been mapped out. It is no surprise, in other words, to find stylistics in a state of disorganization when syntax and semantics, upon which stylistics clearly depends, have themselves been hampered by the lack of a theory that is inclusive, unified, and plausible. . . . Especially damaging is the critic's inability, for lack of a theory, to take into account the deeper structural features of language, precisely those which should enter most revealingly into a stylistic description. *[pp. 425–426]*

Ohmann's reason for thinking that transformational grammar will be of use in remedying this situation is an extremely interesting one:

> . . . the idea of style implies that words on a page might have been different, or differently arranged, without a corresponding difference in substance. . . . Clearly it would help [in supporting our stylistic intuitions] to have a grammar that provided certain relationships, formally statable, of alternativeness among constructions. . . . A generative grammar with a transformational component provides apparatus for breaking down a sentence in a stretch of discourse into underlying kernel sentences (or strings, strictly speaking) and for specifying the grammatical operations that have been performed upon them. It also permits

the analyst to construct, from the same set of kernel sentences, other non-kernel sentences. These may reasonably be thought of as *alternatives* to the original sentence, in that they are simply different constructs out of the identical elementary grammatical units. Thus the idea of alternative phrasings, which is crucial to the notion of style, has a clear analogue within the framework of a transformational grammar. [*pp. 427, 430–431*]

Ohmann then produces four examples to illustrate this thesis. The first two, which are the most important ones, are passages from Faulkner and Hemingway, and Ohmann proposes to alter each of them by reversing the effects of three generalized transformations. (At this stage in the development of transformational syntactic theory, singulary transformations like the passive and question transformations, which operate upon a single sentence and convert it into a new sentence, were opposed to generalized transformations, which operate upon a pair of simple sentences and merge them to form a new complex sentence.) While the Faulkner passage is reduced to something that has no resemblance to its original, the Hemingway passage stays pretty much the same. This leads Ohmann to comment: "it is interesting, and promising, that a stylistic difference so huge as that between the Faulkner and Hemingway passages can be largely explained on the basis of so little grammatical apparatus" (*p. 436*). After considering two more examples, he concludes his essay by observing that

. . . transformational patterns constitute a significant part of what the sensitive reader perceives as style. Transformational analysis of literary discourse promises to the critic stylistic descriptions which are at once simpler and deeper than any hitherto available, and therefore more adequate foundations for critical interpretation. [*pp. 438–439*]

But are these optimistic conclusions justified? It seems to me that they are not. The Faulkner passage comes from the middle of a two-page run-on sentence from "The Bear," replete with conjunctions and relative clauses. Thus two of the generalized transformations Ohmann reverses are the conjunction transformation and the relative clause transformation; it is mainly these two reversals that break the passage up into the underlying kernel sentences, which sound short and choppy and therefore utterly unlike Faulkner. (The third reversal, of the comparative transformation, has considerably less stylistic effect.) Here for example is a bit of Faulkner's original sentence:

> . . . the desk and the shelf above it on which rested the ledgers in which McCaslin recorded the slow outward trickle of food and supplies and equipment which returned each fall as cotton made and ginned and sold . . .[22]

Here is what it becomes when the three transformations are reversed:

> . . . the desk. The shelf was above it. The ledgers rested on the shelf. . . . McCaslin recorded the trickle of food in the ledgers. McCaslin recorded the trickle of supplies in the ledgers. McCaslin recorded the trickle of equipment in the ledgers. The trickle was slow. The trickle was outward. The trickle returned each fall as cotton. The cotton was made. The cotton was ginned. The cotton was sold.

Here on the other hand is part of the Hemingway passage, from the conclusion of the story "Soldier's Home":

> So his mother prayed for him and then they stood up and Krebs kissed his mother and went out of the house. He had tried so to keep his life from being complicated. Still, none of it had touched him. He had felt sorry for his mother and she had made him lie. He would go to Kansas City and get a job and she would feel all right about it. There would be one more scene before he got away. He would not go down to his father's office. He would miss that one.[23]

[22] *Go Down, Moses* (New York: Random House, 1942), pp. 255–256.

[23] *The Fifth Column and the First Forty-Nine Stories* (New York: Scribner's, 1938), pp. 250–251.

The effect of reversing the three generalized transformations is merely to delete the "and's" and replace them by periods. But what does all this grammatical machinery make us see that we did not see before? It seems to me that Ohmann's analyses, like Chatman's, provide nothing more than cumbersome restatements of what we already knew: that Faulkner's style is characterized by long run-on sentences strung together by conjunctions and relatives, while Hemingway's is characterized by short simple sentences that sound rather like kernel sentences. We really learn nothing new; the restatement just looks impressive because it is couched in terms of a scientific theory. The conjunction and relative clause transformations are, *by definition,* the grammatical operations that string together kernel sentences with conjunctions and relatives, and therefore to say that their operation mainly determines the stylistic character of Faulkner's sentence is in no way to explain or support or clarify the intuitive (and directly verifiable) insight that the stylistic character of the sentence is mainly determined by the presence of conjunctions and relatives; it is merely to rephrase that insight.

In Ohmann's statements that "the deeper structural features of language" are "precisely those which should enter most revealingly into a stylistic description," and that the "simpler and deeper" our "stylistic descriptions" are, the more adequately they will reflect "what the sensitive reader perceives as style," we meet again the assumption that the linguist's and the critic's analyses are going in the same direction. But by this time I think we can begin to question that assumption. The characteristics of the Faulkner sentence determined by the operation of the conjunction and relative transformations are "deep" in the sense that these transformations are among the most common and intuitively fundamental to English grammar; but precisely for that reason those characteristics are necessarily very general and superficial so far as the literary critic is concerned. They will be noticed not only by Ohmann's "sensitive reader" but by virtually every reader, and to have noticed them will not take us more deeply—in the critic's sense of that word— into the passage but will leave us virtually where we started, having hardly scratched the surface. A moment's reflection is all it takes to see that one could easily construct a long run-on sentence that shared those characteristics with the Faulkner sentence yet did not sound in the least like Faulkner. If, for example, our constructed sentence dealt with different sorts of objects, was less smoothly cadenced, and made no mention of either the cyclical passing of the seasons or of McCaslin's equally steady recording of supplies in the ledgers, then the characteristically Faulknerian effect of the original sentence—the effect created here, as so often in his work, by an incantatory evocation of a local and personal past linked in some way to the larger processes of nature and history— would be completely lost. In fact it seems that the "simpler and deeper" (in Ohmann's sense of those terms) a "stylistic description" is, the more unrevealing and critically useless it will be. That sort of simplicity and depth are not what the critic is after.

A related point can be made about the Hemingway passage. "Notice that the reduced passage still sounds very much like Hemingway," Ohmann comments after offering his revision. "Nothing has changed that seems crucial to his style" (p. 435). Again the resulting stylistic description seems to me to tell us only uselessly superficial things about the style of the passage, but in this case if we look harder I think we find that something crucial has been lost and that the description is therefore actually false. What is lost is the neutral, nerveless, unemphatic quality of sentences like "So his mother prayed for him and then they stood up and Krebs kissed his mother and went out of the house," sentences that contribute importantly to the creation of a character like Krebs who moves from one action to another as though he were an automaton or were moving in a dream. And this quality is important not just to this passage but to Hemingway's style—insofar as one can ever give a very precise or meaningful general characterization of a writer's style—because this is the sort of character he often wants to create, a character who tries to effect a drastic simplification of an unbearable or dangerous experience by separating himself from it as he acts. ("Still," Krebs reassures himself, "none of it had touched him.") For example, opening a volume of Hemingway's stories at random, to a story I have never read called "After the Storm," I find this:

I hung onto the dinghy and got my breath and then I climbed in and took a couple of breaths and dove again. I swam down and took hold of the edge of the port hole with my fingers and held it and hit the glass as hard as I could with the wrench. I could see the woman floated in the water through the glass. Her hair was tied once close to her head and it floated all out in the water. I could see the rings on one of her hands. She was right up close to the port hole and I hit the glass twice and I didn't even crack it. When I came up I thought I wouldn't make it to the top before I'd have to breathe.

I went down once more and I cracked the glass, only cracked it, and when I came up my nose was bleeding and I stood on the bow of the liner with my bare feet on the letters of her name and my head just out and rested there and then I swam over to the skiff and pulled up into it and sat there waiting for my head to stop aching and looking down into the water glass, but I bled so I had to wash out the water glass. Then I lay back in the skiff and held my hand under my nose to stop it and I lay there with my head back looking up and there was a million birds above and all around.[24]

Here as in the Krebs passage and in many others it would be easy to turn up, the sense of drifting from one action to another as in a dream (or nightmare)

[24] *The Fifth Column and the First Forty-Nine Stories*, pp. 472–473.

is lost if Hemingway's sentences are broken up into the much more emphatic and decisive kernel sentences. As with the Faulkner example, then, the characteristics isolated by Ohmann's analysis are not those that are of interest to the critic trying to describe the style of the passage.

This brief survey of recent attempts to apply linguistics to criticism will do to indicate not only the failure of these writers to come up with anything useful but also the candor with which they have criticized each other and the modesty of the claims they have made for their work. As I said at the beginning of this chapter, Ohmann's remark about the dependence of stylistics upon both syntax and semantics suggests that such efforts may next move in the direction of semantics, and we might pause here for a moment to consider their prospects of success. When we recall Katz's statement, quoted above on page 101, that the linguist working in semantics must restrict himself to talking about "the cognitive content of linguistic constructions as opposed to associated images, emotive overtones, attitudes, recollections, connotations, and metaphorical collations"—as opposed, that is, to some of the most common and important poetic resources of language—these prospects certainly do not appear very bright. But as I also said earlier, I think the really interesting reasons why they are not very bright have more to do with the large theoretical mistake about the nature of critical explanation which I mentioned then than with the particular incidental restriction of Chomskyan semantics to cognitive content. In the work of the linguists this mistake was embodied in the assumption, which we have seen to be invalid, that the analyses of the linguist and the critic are going in the same direction; we can begin to get a clearer idea of what is wrong with that assumption from the early efforts of I. A. Richards to make a very different brand of semantics relevant to criticism.

As I suggested at the beginning of this chapter, these efforts may have been in Harold Whitehall's mind when he made his remark about "semantics, either epistemological or communicative," not being helpful to linguists interested in literature. Yet in many ways Richards' point of departure was very much like that of the linguists. In the first book he wrote on his own, *The Principles of Literary Criticism,* he too deplored the fact that criticism (or at any rate, most recent criticism) was impressionistic. However, his reasons for doing so were different from those of most of the linguists. Richards wrote out of a keen sense that the critic's function was an extremely important one, more difficult to fulfill now than at any previous time:

> With the increase of population the problem presented by the gulf between what is preferred by the majority and what is accepted as excellent by the most qualified opinion has become infinitely more serious and appears likely to become threatening in the near future. For many reasons standards are much more in need of defence than they used to be. It is perhaps premature to envisage a collapse of values, a transvaluation by which popular taste replaces trained discrimination. Yet commercialism has done stranger things . . .[25]

It seemed to Richards that with criticism in its present state, the critic, when asked to justify his opinions, could not offer "reasons of a clear and convincing kind as to why his preferences are worth attention," but could only fall back on snobbery: "The expert in matters of taste is in an awkward position when he differs from the majority. He is forced to say in effect, 'I am better than you. My taste is more refined, my nature more cultured, you will do well to become more like me than you are'" (*pp. 36–37*).

[25] 3rd ed. (New York: Harcourt Brace Jovanovich, 1928; 1st ed., 1925), p. 36.

Thus it was because he thought criticism such a serious business that Richards thought critics needed something better than snobbery to fall back on—that they needed, in fact, principles. It was these he set himself to supply them with; hence the title of his book. Near the beginning he wrote:

Criticism, as I understand it, is the endeavour to discriminate between experiences and to evaluate them. We cannot do this without some understanding of the nature of experience, or without theories of valuation and communication. Such principles as apply in criticism must be taken from these more fundamental studies. All other critical principles are arbitrary, and the history of the subject is a record of their obstructive influence. [p. 2]

And again: "The two pillars upon which a theory of criticism must rest are an account of value and an account of communication" (p. 25). Two years earlier, in 1923, he and C. K. Ogden, attempting in *The Meaning of Meaning* to lay the groundwork for a new science of symbolism, had said at the outset:

The analysis of the process of communication is partly psychological, and psychology has now reached a stage at which this part may be successfully undertaken. Until this had happened the science of Symbolism necessarily remained in abeyance, but there is no longer any excuse for vague talk about Meaning, and ignorance of the ways in which words deceive us.[26]

Therefore it was natural that Richards should turn to psychology for his theories of communication and value.

Just as the linguists whose work we have reviewed assumed that since literature is composed of language, critical remarks are really vague linguistic remarks that require translation into linguistic terms if criticism is to be put upon a firm basis, so Richards assumed that since literature communicates its mean-

[26] 10th ed. (London: Routledge & Kegan Paul, 1949), p. 8.

ings to us by psychological processes, critical remarks —which he defined as remarks "about the values of experiences and the reasons for regarding them as valuable, or not valuable" *(Principles, p. 23)*—are really vague (or even meaningless) remarks about literature's psychological effects which require the corresponding sort of translation:

We are accustomed to say that a picture is beautiful, instead of saying that it causes an experience in us which is valuable in certain ways. The discovery that the remark, "This is beautiful," must be turned round and expanded in this way before it is anything but a mere noise signalling the fact that we approve of the picture, was a great and difficult achievement. Even to-day, such is the insidious power of grammatical forms, the belief that there is such a quality or attribute, namely Beauty, which attaches to the things which we rightly call beautiful, is probably inevitable for all reflective persons at a certain stage of their mental development.

Even among those who have escaped from this delusion and are well aware that we continually talk as though things possess qualities, when what we ought to say is that they cause effects in us of one kind or another, the fallacy of "projecting" the effect and making it a quality of its cause tends to recur. . . .

We must be prepared then to translate, into phrases pedantic and uncouth, all the too simple utterances which the conversational decencies exact. . . . We shall endeavor in what follows to show that critical remarks are merely a branch of psychological remarks, and that no special ethical or metaphysical ideas need be introduced to explain value. *[Principles, pp. 20–23]*

Moreover, the critical terms that Richards picked out as especially in need of translation were remarkably similar to those that interest the linguists:

Such terms as "construction" "form," "balance," "composition," "design," "unity," "expression," for all the arts; as "depth," "movement," "texture," "solidity," in the criticism of painting; as "rhythm," "stress," "plot," "character," in literary criticism; as "harmony," "atmosphere," "development," in music, are instances. All these terms are currently used as though they stood for qualities inherent in things outside the mind, as a painting, in the sense of an assemblage of pigments, is undoubtedly outside the mind. [*Principles*, p. 21]

There are many things in these paragraphs that remind us not only of the linguists but also (and perhaps more directly) of Korzybski: the intense concern to distinguish things outside the mind from those inside it, the talk of "delusion" and "projecting," the contention that these are the "inevitable" bad results of "the insidious power of grammatical forms," and of course the faith that translating (or at least being prepared to translate) our ordinary language into the language of some scientific theory will automatically bring a gain in precision and set us free. Certainly after reading them we are in no doubt as to why Richards' early work had a strong influence on general semanticists. Moreover, behind Richards' theory of communication lies a theory of meaning that is very much like that of Hayakawa and Chase, and of Bloomfield as well. But this theory, and particularly the whole matter of "emotive meaning," have been dealt with so well and so often[27] that I shall say nothing about them here, but rather turn immediately to Richards' "two pillars," his theories of communication and value.

Nor need these detain us long. The theory of communication, as Ogden and Richards first stated it, was simply that "a language transaction or a communication may be defined as a use of symbols in such a way that acts of reference occur in a hearer which are similar in all relevant respects to those which are

[27] Perhaps the two best discussions are Max Black's "Ogden and Richards' Theory of Interpretation" and "Questions about Emotive Meaning," both reprinted in *Language and Philosophy* (Ithaca, N.Y.: Cornell University Press, 1949), pp. 189–200 and 203–220, respectively. In connection with the latter essay, see also Richards' "Emotive Meaning Again," reprinted in his collection *Speculative Instruments* (Chicago: University of Chicago Press, 1955), pp. 39–56.

symbolized by them in the speaker" *(Meaning of Meaning, pp. 205–206)*. Or as Richards later expressed it (in slightly different terms):

> . . . communication defined as strict transference of or participation in identical experiences does not occur. . . .
>
> All that occurs is that, under certain conditions, separate minds have closely similar experiences. . . . Communication, we shall say, takes place when one mind so acts upon its environment that another mind is influenced, and in that other mind an experience occurs which is like the experience in the first mind, and is caused in part by that experience. *[Principles, pp. 176–177]*

But if the statement that communication occurs when one mind has an experience similar to and in part caused by an experience in another mind is to tell us anything useful—if, that is, it is to be more than just an arbitrary definition of communication—there must be some way of examining the two experiences and of ascertaining their similarity. Richards never tells us how to do this, however, and in fact we never attempt to do anything like it when we want to find out whether or not we have communicated something to somebody. Also, the word "similar," left standing by itself, is (as we have seen before) a notorious question-beggar since anything can be thought of as similar to anything else in some respect or other. Finally, it is hard even to know what the theory is denying (and hence what it is asserting) since it is hard to know what it would mean for two minds to participate in "identical experiences." Richards' statement that they never do so seems less like an empirical statement about what does or does not happen than like a logical or conceptual statement about the meaning of the word "identical" or our use of the concept of identity.

Now one reason Richards thought a theory of criticism presupposed a theory of communication was that he thought that "the arts are the supreme form of the communicative activity" and that "it is as a communicator that it is most profitable to consider the artist" *(Principles, p. 26)*. Yet the difficulties of his theory of communication are only compounded when the communication situation in question is the situation of reading a poem or looking at a picture or listening to a piece of music. "The degree to which [the work of art] accords with the relevant experience of the artist is a measure of the degree to which it will arouse similar experiences in others" *(Principles, p. 27)*, he tells us. But then, a few pages later, he candidly admits that "nearly all speculations as to what went on in the artist's mind are unverifiable" *(Principles, p. 30)*. Thus the definition of a poem which he proposes near the end of his book, by way of answering what he had initially asserted to be one of "the fundamental questions which criticism is required to answer" *(Principles, p. 6)*, is hopelessly tangled:

This, although it may seem odd and complicated, is by far the most convenient, in fact it is the only workable way of defining a poem; namely, as a class of experiences which do not differ in any character more than a certain amount, varying for each character, from a standard experience. We may take as this standard experience the relevant experience of the poet when contemplating the completed composition.

Anyone whose experience approximates in this degree to the standard experience will be able to judge the poem and his remarks about it will be about some experience which is included in the class. Thus we have what we want, a sense, namely, in which a critic can be said to have not read the poem or to have misread it. *[Principles, pp. 226–227]*

But what good does it do us to have "a sense" in which a critic can be said to have misread a poem—to have, that is, just another (and more cumbersome) way of saying he has misread it—if we don't have an empirical criterion (that we didn't have before) for discovering whether or not he has in fact misread it?

No more good, it would seem, than did those restatements offered by Chatman and Ohmann of critical insights that we could already state perfectly well for ourselves in ordinary language. Moreover, we can see the impossibility of applying Richards' definition to attain such an empirical criterion when we note that besides the difficulties mentioned before, new ones are raised by his use of expressions like "character," "certain amount," "standard," and "relevant." Certainly a poet's experience "when contemplating the completed composition" seems in practice to be even more inaccessible than Garland Cannon's "recording of a poet reading his work only moments after he had finished composing it." But even if we could somehow (and in some sense or other) have access to that experience, how could we possibly know what parts of it were "relevant" and hence to be taken as comprising the "standard experience"? Or what the "certain amount" of allowed variation was? Or what was to count as a "character"? Or how much the "certain amount" of allowed variation could itself "vary" for "each character"? Finally it seems just plain odd to think of a poem as "a class of experiences," even if we could fix the limits of that class (as we cannot do in the case of Richards' definition). The distinction between a poem and anyone's experience of it seems intuitively as much worth preserving as did the distinction between a poem and anyone's oral performance of it, or (to recall de Saussure's analogy) the distinction between a symphony and its performances.

The other of Richards' "two pillars," his theory of value, is open to some of the same objections as his theory of communication. "We may start," he writes, "from the fact that impulses may be divided into appetencies and aversions, and begin by saying that anything is valuable which satisfies an appetency or 'seeking after' "; and a page later he offers a qualification: "We can now extend our definition. Anything is valuable which will satisfy an appetency without involving the frustration of some equal or *more important* appetency" *(Principles, pp. 47–48)*. Then, since "a growing order is the principle of the mind," he concludes that "The importance of an impulse ... can be defined for our purposes as *the extent of the disturbance of other impulses in the individual's activities which the thwarting of the impulse involves" (Principles, pp. 50–51)*. Finally he writes:

> What is good or valuable, we have said, is the exercise of impulses and the satisfaction of their appetencies. When we say that anything is good we mean that it satisfies, and by a good experience we mean one in which the impulses which make it are fulfilled and successful, adding as the necessary qualification that their exercise and satisfaction shall not interfere in any way with more important impulses. *[Principles, p. 58]*

Now the move from saying that anything which satisfies an appetency is good or valuable to saying that all we *mean* when we say something is good or valuable is that it satisfies an appetency is not as innocent as it looks. In fact it involves Richards in important logical difficulties; but these have been so thoroughly discussed (though not in connection with Richards) that I need not go into them here.[28] For our purposes it is enough to note that the usefulness of the theory of value, like that of the theory of communication, depends on the relevant inner experiences—in this case our appetencies and aversions —being empirically accessible, and on our (or someone else's) being able to measure their importance and satisfaction just as we can measure our own body

---

[28] The logical difficulties I am referring to are those associated with what in moral philosophy is called "naturalism" or "the naturalistic fallacy." Their classic treatment is in G. E. Moore's *Principia Ethica* (Cambridge: Cambridge University Press, 1903); a more satisfactory recent treatment may be found in R. M. Hare's *The Language of Morals* (Oxford: Oxford University Press, 1952).

temperature or blood pressure (or someone else can measure them for us). But here too Richards gives us no way of making the relevant measurements, and just as we never actually do try to measure the similarity of two inner experiences (whatever that would mean) to find out if communication has taken place, so too if we are trying to analyze or evaluate a poem we never try to measure that "resolution, inter-inanimation, and balancing of impulses" in terms of which Richards asserts that "all the most valuable effects of poetry must be described" *(Principles, p. 113)*.

Even more important than the specific content (or lack of content) of these two theories is the fact that when Richards comes to deal with a particular poem, he, unlike the linguists, usually makes no attempt either to apply his theories or to use the cumbersome terminology that goes with them. This is especially true in *Practical Criticism,* which seems to me his best book precisely because it is the one in which he had to deal most often with particular poems. Take just one of his excellent (though all too few) analyses as an example. In a chapter on figurative language he is attempting to correct some of the misconceptions of the students whose "protocols" (as he called their submitted comments on the poems) make up the bulk of the early portion of the book. The question at issue is whether the "literalism" represented by the students' objections to the use of personification and the allegedly mixed metaphors in the opening three stanzas of one of the poems is the sort "which would be fatal to nearly all poetry" or is rather "the legitimate variety, aimed at the abuse, not at the use, of figurative language."[29] The stanzas, by G. H. Luce, run as follows:

> **Climb, cloud, and pencil all the blue**
> **With your miraculous stockade;**

[29] (London: Routledge & Kegan Paul, 1929), p. 198. See B. A. O. Williams' review in *Mind,* LXVII (1958), 409–411.

> The earth will have her joy of you
>> And limn your beauty till it fade.
>
> Puzzle the cattle at the grass
>> And paint your pleasure on their flanks;
> Shoot, as the ripe cornfield you pass,
>> A shudder down those golden ranks.
>
> On wall and window slant your hand
>> And sidle up the garden stair;
> Cherish each flower in all the land
>> With soft encroachments of cool air.

In order to show that "sometimes personification allows us to say compendiously and clearly what would be extraordinarily difficult to say without it," Richards comments:

> . . . the bending of the cloud shadow as it passes from the surface of the earth to the upright plane of "wall and window" is given at once by "slant your hand." The changed angle of incidence thus noted adds a solidity and particularity to the effect described, and since vividness is a large part of the intention of the poem at this point, the means employed should not be overlooked. Of course, if "hand" be read to mean a part of the cloud itself and not as the extremity of a limb of the cloud's shadow, the image becomes merely silly, and some of the condemnations in the protocols are explained if not excused.
>
> So, too, with "sidle"; it gives the accidental, oblique quality of the movement of the shadow, and gives it in a single word by means of a single particularising scene. [*Practical Criticism, p. 200*]

And a few pages later he replies to the protocol-writers who had found the metaphors mixed:

> "Pencil," if we take it to mean "produce the effects of pencilling" (such are the exigencies of paraphrasing) hardly mixes the metaphor in any serious fashion. Its suggestion both of the hard, clear outline of the cloud's edge and of the shadowy variations in the lighting of its inner recesses, is not in the least cancelled by "climb" or by the sky-scraper hoist of "miraculous stockade." . . . "Puzzle" has accuracy also on its side against these cavillers. Anyone who watches the restless shift of cattle as the shadow suddenly darkens their world for them will endorse the poet's

observation. But if the cows never noticed any change of light the word would still be justified through its evocative effect upon men. Similarly with "paint" and "shoot"; they work as a rapid and fresh notation of not very unfamiliar effects, and there is no reason to suppose that those readers for whom they are successful are in any way damaging or relaxing their sensibility. *[Practical Criticism, pp. 202–203]*

The point about these comments is not merely that they are not couched in terms of appetencies and aversions, that they do not in any way refer to or depend on Richards' particular theories; the point is also that they seem entirely remote from the world of theories, general criteria, critical principles, formulable norms for judgment, and so on. Indeed, an important part of Richards' aim here as in the rest of the book is to expose the inadequacy of the general principles or theories about poetry which got in the way of his students and kept them from responding adequately to the poems he set before them. But neither here nor at most other points when he talks effectively about a particular poem or about the process of reading is his main concern to supply better general principles or theories to supplant those of his students. Ohmann, we recall, thought that we must have "a full and convincing explication of the notion of style" in order to describe particular styles accurately and objectively; similarly, Richards tells us early in *Principles* that answering "preliminary questions" like "What *is* a picture, a poem, a piece of music? How can experiences be compared? What is value?" is "required in order to approach" questions like "What gives the experience of reading a certain poem its value?" *(pp. 5–6)*. But in the analysis of the poem about the cloud, when he tries to explain why he thinks the figurative language is effectively used and should not have been condemned by the protocol-writers, he does not do so by invoking some general criterion or rule for telling good from bad figurative language. Nor, we might also note, does he find himself condemned by the lack of such a criterion to fall back on snobbery, condemned merely to assert "I am better than you. My taste is more refined, my nature more cultured, you will do well to become more like me than you are." Instead he gives us his reasons for thinking as he does by pointing to the various words and images of the poem, specifying the evocative qualities they take on from the poem's subject-matter and the ways in which these qualities enable them in turn to reinforce and embody that subject-matter.

To put the point more generally: despite his earlier claim that the "reasons of a clear and convincing kind" which the critic needs in order to show "why his preferences are worth attention" must be derived from general theories of communication and value, the triviality of his own theories does not at all leave Richards at a loss to supply reasons for his particular judgment. Moreover, the reasons he gives seem perfectly clear, whether or not we find them absolutely convincing and agree with him about the poem. There isn't really anything "subjective" or "impressionistic" about this sort of writing. Certainly Richards is stating his impressions of the poem, but by anchoring them in particular verbal details he makes us able to recreate those impressions for ourselves and share them, and thus in an important sense they become public property.

In view of the gap between Richards' theories and his critical practice, it is interesting that towards the end of *Practical Criticism* he seems repeatedly to repudiate the whole notion of judging poetry by general theories or critical principles of any sort:

The more refined and discriminating our preconception of poetry is, the more impossible any *direct* application becomes. . . . For the more thoroughly we work out our account of the differences between good and bad poetry the more intricate and complex the account becomes. Alternatives, conditions, qualifications, compensating conditions . . . and the rest, force themselves into it under the pressure of the facts, until it becomes evident that a direct practical application of an adequate account to any poem is impossible. . . .

Any general theory that we may be tempted to apply to poetry and continue to apply, must—unless we are very Napoleonic readers—be of the kind which disguises great vagueness and ambiguity behind an appearance of simplicity and precision. . . .

All critical doctrines are attempts to convert choice into what may seem a safer activity—the reading [of] evidence and the application of rules and principles. . . .

Thus no theory, no description, of poetry can be trusted which is not too intricate to be applied. . . .

When we have the poem in all its minute particulars as intimately and as fully present to our minds as we can contrive—no general description of it but the very experience itself present as a living pulse in our biographies—then our acceptance or rejection of it must be *direct*. There comes a point in all criticism where a sheer choice has to be made without the support of any arguments, principles, or general rules. All that arguments or principles can do is to protect us from irrelevancies, red-herrings and disturbing preconceptions. . . . They may preserve us from bad arguments but they cannot supply good ones. [*pp. 298–299, 300, 301, 302, 302–303*]

Though Richards is here ostensibly talking only about the particular "technical presuppositions and critical preconceptions" of his protocol-writers, the sweep and eloquence of his language suggest that for the moment at any rate, under the pressure of describing directly the complexities of the process of critical reading, he perhaps also half-realized the futility of his own efforts to establish a science of criticism. One can only regret that these paragraphs from *Practical Criticism* did not constitute the turning-point in Richards' career that they might have done, but they do offer more than a mere repudiation of any possible theory of criticism: rather, it seems to me that taken in the context of Richards' critical practice, they contain hints towards a better sort of theory, one that explains the failures of the linguists whose work we reviewed earlier.

III

Oddly enough, the critic who has most successfully developed these hints is perhaps of all important contemporary critics the one most fiercely opposed to all theorizing, F. R. Leavis. Though the two essays in which Leavis has dealt importantly with these matters are readily accessible, they do not seem to be as widely known as they should be; therefore I shall quote from both of them at some length.

The first is an essay called "Literary Studies," which originally appeared in Leavis' magazine *Scrutiny* and was later incorporated into his book *Education and the University*. The essay is intended as a corrective not only to traditional ways of teaching English literature but also to the work of certain modern critics, including Richards. After referring disparagingly to Richards' "ambition to make [critical] analysis a laboratory technique,"[30] Leavis writes:

> In criticism, of course (one would emphasize), nothing can be proved; there can, in the nature of the case, be no laboratory-demonstration or anything like it. Nevertheless, it is nearly always possible to go further than merely asserting a judgment or inviting agreement with a general account. Commonly one can call attention to this, that or the other detail by way of making the nature and force of one's judgment plain. [*Education and the University, p. 74*]

While this statement directly contradicts the assumption, common to Richards and the linguists, that the *reasons* a critic gives for his judgments must be derived from a scientific *theory* of some sort, it perfectly accords with what we saw to be Richards' actual practice in dealing with the poem about the cloud. And a fuller statement earlier in Leavis' essay is perhaps even more relevant to *Practical Criticism:*

> Analysis, one would go on, is the process by which we seek to

[30] *Education and the University* (London: Chatto & Windus, 1943), p. 72.

attain a complete reading of the poem—a reading that approaches as nearly as possible to the perfect reading. There is about it nothing in the nature of "murdering to dissect," and suggestions that it can be anything in the nature of laboratory-method misrepresent it entirely. We can have the poem only by an inner kind of possession; it is "there" for analysis only in so far as we are responding appropriately to the words on the page. . . . Analysis is not a dissection of something that is already and passively there. What we call analysis is, of course, a constructive or creative process. It is a more deliberate following-through of that process of creation in response to the poet's words which reading is. It is a re-creation in which, by a considering attentiveness, we ensure a more than ordinary faithfulness and completeness. [*Education and the University, p. 70*]

Leavis' stress on critical analysis as a "constructive or creative process" again accurately describes what Richards did with the poem about the cloud, and the phrase "an inner kind of possession" echoes Richards' point about the necessity of having "the poem in all its minute particulars as intimately and fully present to our minds as we can contrive."

That critical analysis is a process of imagining or working one's way into something rather than of applying general criteria to it from the outside is stated even more fully and illuminatingly by Leavis in the other of his two essays. Shortly after the appearance of Leavis' book *Revaluation*,[31] a very selective critical survey of English poetry from the Metaphysicals through the Romantics, the aesthetician and literary historian René Wellek wrote a letter to *Scrutiny* in which he said he wished "you [i.e., Leavis] had stated your assumptions more explicitly and defended them systematically." Wellek went on to sketch what he called "your ideal of poetry, your 'norm' with which you measure every poet," and invited Leavis "to defend this position more abstractly and to become conscious that large ethical, philosophical, and, of course, ultimately, also aesthetic *choices*

[31] (London: Chatto & Windus, 1936).

are involved." In his reply, which was also first printed in *Scrutiny*,[32] Leavis first took issue with what he called "the judicial, one-eye-on-the-standard approach suggested by Dr. Wellek's phrase: 'your "norm" with which you measure every poet,'" and then he described the critical process in terms that made it clear why he thought such an approach inappropriate:

Words in poetry invite us not to "think about" and judge, but to "feel into" or "become"—to realize a complex experience that is given in the words. . . . The critic—the reader of poetry—is indeed concerned with evaluation, but to figure him as measuring with a norm which he brings up to the object and applies from the outside is to misrepresent the process. The critic's aim is, first, to realize as sensitively and completely as possible this or that which claims his attention; and a certain valuing is implicit in the realizing. As he matures in experience of the new thing he asks, explicitly and implicitly: "Where does this come? How does it stand in relation to . . . ? How relatively important does it seem?" And the organization into which it settles as a constituent in becoming "placed" is an organization of similarly "placed" things, things that have found their bearings with regard to one another, and not a theoretical system or a system determined by abstract considerations. . . . He doesn't ask, "How does this accord with these specifications of goodness in poetry?"; he aims to make fully conscious and articulate the immediate sense of value that "places" the poem. *[Importance of Scrutiny, pp. 31–32]*

Therefore, though Leavis conceded that "it should, of course, be possible to elicit principles and abstractly formulable norms" from the "consistency and . . . coherence of response" that the critic seeks to attain and articulate, he added:

If, as I did, I avoided such generalities, it was not out of

---

[32] Leavis reprinted his reply in *The Common Pursuit* (London: Chatto & Windus, 1952), pp. 211–222; but I shall quote from Eric Bentley (ed.), *The Importance of Scrutiny* (New York: Grove Press [1957]), since both Wellek's original letter and Leavis' reply appear there together, pp. 23–40.

timidity; it was because they seemed too clumsy to be of any use. I thought I had provided something better. My whole effort was to work in terms of concrete judgements and particular analyses: "This—doesn't it?—bears such a relation to that; this kind of thing—don't you find it so?—wears better than that," etc. [Importance of Scrutiny, pp. 33–34]

And finally, quoting some of the phrases that Wellek had elicited from *Revaluation* and included in his "sketch" of Leavis' "norm," Leavis concluded his defense:

I feel that by own methods I have attained a relative precision that makes this summarizing seem intolerably clumsy and inadequate. I do not, again, argue in general terms that there should be "no emotion for its own sake, no afflatus, no mere generous emotionality, no luxury in pain or joy"; but by choice, arrangement, and analysis of concrete examples I give those phrases (in so far, that is, as I have achieved my purpose) a precision of meaning they couldn't have got in any other way. [Importance of Scrutiny, p. 34]

I think it is most significant that the arguments Leavis used against a traditional aesthetician like Wellek are so similar to the ones he used against Richards' attempts at a science of criticism, for it seems to me that Richards' assumptions about criticism, and also those of the linguists, are really very similar to some basic assumptions of traditional aesthetics. Traditional aestheticians too have contended that critical remarks, in their present customary form, are vague, and that the principles implicit in them must receive explicit statement if criticism is ever to become respectably objective. These theorists have differed from Richards and the linguists in that they have not sought to import these principles from an already existing science such as psychology or linguistics but rather to establish them inductively, by an examination of criticism or of works of art or of both, so as to constitute an independent body of knowledge. Though there is not much of this sort of aesthetics written these days—and for that we surely have Richards to thank—a book of it still appears now and then. Harold Osborne begins his recent *Aesthetics and Criticism* from a position similar to Wellek's:

> It will be our concern to show that every formulation of doctrine, every casual remark about the critic's function, indeed every assay of practical criticism, inevitably and inescapably implies theoretical assumptions which belong to the province of aesthetics; and therefore so long as aesthetics remains inchoate, criticism must needs be muddled and confused. . . .
>
> There can be no single judgement of practical criticism which does not involve latent doctrines of aesthetics. And if your aesthetics is bad, whether it be overt or implied, your criticism cannot well evitate futility. . . .
>
> For unless the critic defines his norms of judgement clearly and without ambivalence, either by verbal description or ostensively, the judgements which he utters will be strictly devoid of meaning, they will be no more than empty ejaculations.[33]

And then of course there are the curious efforts of Northrop Frye, located somewhere between traditional aesthetics and the work of Richards and the linguists, to make criticism systematic by supplying it with "a coordinating principle, a central hypothesis which, like the theory of evolution in biology, will see the phenomena it deals with as parts of a whole."[34]

What all these writers share, and what seems to me to invalidate most of what they have to say about criticism, is the misconception about critical explanation which I referred to at the beginning of this chapter. As will by now be clear, the linguists, Richards, and traditional aestheticians like Wellek—whatever their other differences—all assume that the precision or finality that is needed to give critical remarks the desired objectivity is equivalent to generality. I think the reason they do so is that they (consciously or

[33] (London: Routledge & Kegan Paul, 1955), pp. 6, 26, 35.
[34] *Anatomy of Criticism* (Princeton, N.J.: Princeton University Press, 1957), p. 16.

unconsciously) assimilate critical to scientific explanation: what they really mean when they imply (or assert) that the critic's and the linguist's or psychologist's or aesthetician's explanations or analyses are heading in the same direction is that both are heading towards generality. Or it might be better to say that they assimilate critical explanation to what most of us laymen think of as scientific explanation, for the actual intricacies of scientific explanation—of how explanations within one science differ from one another and from those in other sciences—are very difficult matters that can only be handled by philosophers of science. The reason these intricacies (fortunately) need not concern us here is that the literary theorists we have been dealing with are laymen rather than philosophers of science.

For our purposes it will do to say that when we think of the way science explains natural phenomena, we think of it as doing so by bringing them under some theory or by seeing them as instances covered by some causal law. And of course the more general the explanation is, the more powerful and illuminating it is. Thus, for example, if someone asks why full water pipes sometimes burst in winter, we can answer that they always do so when the temperature drops below freezing. This is all right as far as it goes, but it does raise the further question of why they should always burst when the temperature drops below freezing. That question we of course can answer by saying that water always expands when it freezes, but we again might be asked why, in which case we should probably try to say something about the structure of the water molecule.[35] The point is that while it would

[35] I have taken these examples from John Hospers, who uses them to make a different point in his essay, "What is Explanation?," in Antony Flew (ed.), *Essays in Conceptual Analysis* (London: Macmillan, 1956), pp. 102–103. See also Chapters I–III of Daniel M. Taylor, *Explanation and Meaning: An Introduction to Philosophy* (Cambridge: Cambridge University Press, 1970).

not be correct to say that our third answer is the only real answer to the original question, the fact that it is the most general answer tends to make us feel it is the best and most satisfying one. But should this criterion of generality be applied to explanations in all fields of inquiry? At the close of the preceding chapter I tried to suggest tentatively that Katz was perhaps mistaken in applying it to the explanations offered by ordinary language philosophers; I think the material we have reviewed so far in this chapter clearly indicates that it most certainly does not apply to critical explanations.

What then *are* critical explanations like? How do they differ from scientific explanations? As I suggested at the beginning of this chapter, this mistaken view of them is linked to a mistaken view of the way in which certain central concepts function in criticism. The essay I have found most helpful in pointing the way towards a better characterization of critical explanations is one that sets out to examine the functioning of these concepts, an essay by the philosopher Frank Sibley called "Aesthetic Concepts."[36] Sibley begins by distinguishing between two kinds of remarks that may be made about works of art:

We say that a novel has a great number of characters and deals with life in a manufacturing town; that a painting uses pale

---

[36] *The Philosophical Review*, LXVIII (1959), 421–450. See also Vincent Tomas, "Aesthetic Vision," *The Philosophical Review*, LXVIII (1959), 52–67, and Sibley's reply, "Aesthetics and the Looks of Things," *The Journal of Philosophy*, LVI (1959), 905–915; H. G. R. Schwyzer, "Sibley's Aesthetic Concepts," and Sibley's "Aesthetic Concepts: A Rejoinder," *The Philosophical Review*, LXXII (1963), 72–83; Sibley's "Aesthetic and Nonaesthetic," *The Philosophical Review*, LXXIV (1965), 135–159; his contribution to the "Symposium: About Taste," in *The British Journal of Aesthetics*, VI (1966), 68–69; his paper "Colours," *Proceedings of the Aristotelian Society* (New Series), LXVIII (1967–1968), 145–166; and his discussion with Michael Tanner, "Objectivity and Aesthetics," *Proceedings of the Aristotelian Society*, Supplementary XLII (1968), 31–72.

colors, predominantly blues and greens, and has kneeling figures in the foreground; that the theme in a fugue is inverted at such a point and that there is a stretto at the close; that the action of a play takes place in the span of one day and that there is a reconciliation scene in the fifth act. Such remarks may be made by, and such features pointed out to, anyone with normal eyes, ears, and intelligence. On the other hand, we also say that a poem is tightly-knit or deeply moving; that a picture lacks balance, or has a certain serenity and repose, or that the grouping of the figures sets up an exciting tension; that the characters in a novel never really come to life, or that a certain episode strikes a false note. The making of such remarks as these requires the exercise of taste, perceptiveness, or sensitivity, of aesthetic discrimination or appreciation. Accordingly, when a word or expression is such that taste or perceptiveness is required in order to apply it, I shall call it an *aesthetic* term or expression, and I shall, correspondingly, speak of *aesthetic* concepts or taste concepts. *[p. 421]*

He then goes on to point out that while we often support our application of an aesthetic term by using another aesthetic term, as for example when we say that a painting "has an extraordinary vitality because of its free and vigorous style of drawing," we often supply such support by using a non-aesthetic term, by referring to a feature of the work in question which can be recognized without exercising taste or sensitivity. Moreover, Sibley contends, it is always legitimate to ask for an explanation of the latter sort since "aesthetic words apply ultimately because of, and aesthetic qualities ultimately depend upon, the presence of features which, like curving or angular lines, color contrasts, placing of masses, or speed of movement, are visible, audible, or otherwise discernible without any exercise of taste or sensibility" *(p. 424)*.

Most of the remainder of Sibley's essay is concerned with characterizing this dependence of aesthetic terms on non-aesthetic features. Obviously it is not the sort of dependence that exists between a term like "square" and the set of necessary and sufficient conditions for applying it: "For whereas each square is square in virtue of the *same* set of conditions, four equal sides and four right angles, aesthetic terms apply to widely varied objects; one thing is graceful because of these features, another because of those, and so on almost endlessly" *(p. 424)*. Nor is this dependence the sort we find with a term like "intelligent" or "lazy," where there are no necessary conditions for application but there are conditions such that a sufficient number of them will warrant application of the term: "Being a good chess player can count only *towards* and not *against* intelligence" *(p. 425)*, whereas features like slimness and lightness "can be said, at best, to count only *typically* or *characteristically* towards delicacy; they do not count towards in the same sense as condition-features count towards laziness or intelligence" *(p. 428)*. Therefore "no description however full, even in terms characteristic of gracefulness, puts it beyond question that something is graceful in the way a description may put it beyond question that someone is lazy or intelligent" *(p. 429)*. Aesthetic terms or features, Sibley concludes, can be governed only negatively by conditions: "For instance, it may be impossible that a thing should be garish if all its colors are pale pastels, or flamboyant if all its lines are straight. There may be, that is, descriptions using only non-aesthetic terms which are incompatible with descriptions employing certain aesthetic terms" *(pp. 426–427)*.

The relevance for us of Sibley's essay lies first of all in the fact that it is precisely the presence in critical writing of what he calls aesthetic terms which raises suspicions that criticism is, at least in its present condition, subjective, and that it requires a scientific basis of some sort. The list of terms that Richards wants to eliminate from criticism by translating them into psychological terms, quoted above on page 144, is strikingly like Sibley's list of aesthetic terms. Also, as we have seen, it is aesthetic concepts like the design or unity of a work, or the exuberance or placidity of a writer's style, that the linguists are trying to define, or at least to analyze more fully, in terms of the phonemic or syntactic features of a literary text. But of course the idea that such translations and analyses are even possible (let alone desirable or helpful) rests firmly on the assumption Sibley is attacking, the assumption that aesthetic terms are positively condition-governed to some degree or other. For in trying to specify the psychological states or linguistic features that are always or characteristically present when we apply such terms correctly, and that are directly responsible for our applying them, Richards and the linguists are trying precisely to specify the conditions that govern their application, to state the general rules that tell us when to apply them to a particular case. Therefore if Sibley is right about the logic of aesthetic concepts, and it seems to me that he is, I do not see how we can escape the conclusion that the reason the efforts of Richards and the linguists have yielded nothing in the way of positive results is simply that these efforts are radically misdirected. It is important to understand that if this is indeed the case, then the failure of these efforts is not due to the failings of the particular psychological or linguistic theories on which they are based. We therefore have no reason to hope that the development of more adequate theories will bring success in the future; on the contrary, the explanatory adequacy (or for that matter, the lack of it) which a particular scientific theory possesses in its own sphere would seem to have nothing whatever to do with its inapplicability to criticism.

Most writers who have dealt with the theory of criticism have been very much preoccupied with questions of value and with the move that the critic makes from observation and description to evaluation; and since values are linked in many people's minds with subjectivity, it is this preoccupation that has been largely responsible for the assumption that criticism in its present form is subjective and therefore unsatisfactory. The stress that Richards and the linguists lay on value and evaluation in some of the passages I have quoted from them makes it clear, I think, that this is true in their cases even though they are primarily interested in elucidating what Sibley calls aesthetic terms rather than out-and-out value-words like "good." Sibley's emphasis, as we have seen, is not on evaluation but rather on the move from perceiving those qualities of an object which require only normal senses and intelligence to perceiving those which, though dependent on the former sort, are not necessarily perceptible at once but require trained sensitivity and discrimination. "The two questions," he writes, "need separating: the relation of non-aesthetic features . . . to aesthetic qualities, and the relation of aesthetic qualities to 'aesthetically good' (verdicts). Most writings which touch on the nature of aesthetic concepts have this other (verdict) question mainly in mind" *(p. 435n.)*. Moreover, his analysis makes it clear that aesthetic terms are really quite different from the value-words to which other writers have assimilated them. Of course there is some overlap—unity in a work of art is, we say, a good thing—and the relations between the two kinds of terms have not been sufficiently investigated, but it does seem clear that some aesthetic terms are ordinarily used neutrally, without any particular burden of value attaching to them, and that some terms that seem to have a particular burden of value most firmly attached to them can be used with quite opposite implications and yet without strain or oddity. For example, in *The New Yorker* of May 6, 1967, the art critic Harold Rosenberg speaks of Jackson Pollock's painting "Blue Poles" as being "attractive because of a degree of naturalistic grossness" *(p. 170)*.

The effect of Sibley's shift of emphasis, which seems to me to constitute the real originality of his essay, is thus at least partially to remove the taint of subjectivism from criticism by breaking up the old assimi-

lation of criticism to moral or quasi-moral evaluation
and of aesthetic terms to value-words. By redirecting
our attention from criticism as primarily evaluative
to criticism as the attempt to communicate and stimu-
late a special and imaginatively heightened sort of
perception, Sibley in fact brings out the peculiar
objectivity of aesthetic qualities. "It is true that someone with perfect eyes or ears might miss them," he
writes, "but we do after all say we *observe* or *notice*
them ('Did you notice how very graceful she was?'
'Did you observe the exquisite balance in all his pictures?')" *(p. 438)*. Without necessarily subscribing to
the common linkage of values and subjectivity, we
can nonetheless agree that it would seem very odd to
speak of observing how good the poem was or of
noticing the painting's badness.

Sibley's essay thus suggests both that the alleged
subjectivism of aesthetic terms cannot be cleared up
in the way Richards and the linguists propose, by
discovering the general conditions for their application, and that the terms are not really subjective in
the first place. As I said earlier, I think it also suggests
a new and better view of critical explanations. Sibley's contention that the dependence of an object's
aesthetic qualities on its non-aesthetic qualities is
ultimate implies that after the critic has used every
means at his command—including analogy, gesture,
imaginative illustration, and so on—to call our attention to the qualities of the object which seem to him
to justify the application of the aesthetic term in
question, there is no further *kind* of explanation we
can ask for. Critical explanations are therefore quite
different from scientific or quasi-scientific explanations of already perceived phenomena in terms of
some general theory or causal law—explanations of
why water pipes may burst in winter, or of why we
have eclipses of the sun, or of why native speakers
of English will feel there is something queer about
the sentence "The paint is silent." One consequence

of Sibley's conclusion that aesthetic terms are only negatively condition-governed, we recall, is that no description of a particular work, no matter how complete it may be, can ever put it beyond question that a given aesthetic term is applicable to that work. Now if we assume that critical explanations are like what I have been loosely calling scientific explanations, there is a strong temptation to think that it would somehow be better to be able to explain why a particular object possesses this or that aesthetic quality by citing an established precise generalization that all objects possessing certain non-aesthetic qualities possessed by the object also possess the aesthetic quality in question. But what Sibley is saying is that such precise generalizations are unattainable—and again it is worth emphasizing that they are not just practically unattainable, owing to some lack in our present knowledge or some imprecision of our present methods, say, but logically unattainable, unattainable because of the nature of the concepts we are working with and the kind of thing we are trying to explain. Therefore the best or most precise or most conclusive sort of critical explanation usually takes the form of a description, direct or indirect, of a particular work's already perceived non-aesthetic qualities rather than of a generalization about all or most works possessing some non-aesthetic quality or qualities. "We say that [a work of art] is delicate," writes Sibley, "not simply because it is in pale colors but because of *those* pale colors, that it is graceful not because its outline curves slightly but because of *that* particular curve" (p. 434).

When the critic takes us into a work, and tries to get us to see what he sees, he is thus doing something very different from what the linguist or psychologist or other scientist is doing when he brings observed phenomena under a theory or law and thus renders them more fully intelligible than they were before; and of course the insight or trained sensitivity that enables the critic to see more in a work than the lay-

man, and to explain what he sees, is very different
from the knowledge that enables a scientist to explain
particular phenomena. Thus there is no reason why
the critic's analysis should go in the same direction
as the scientific or quasi-scientific sort of analysis
practiced or desired by Richards, the linguists, and
traditional aestheticians like Wellek. The assumption
that it does (or ought to) seems to me merely another
manifestation of what Wittgenstein once memorably
called "our craving for generality."[37] And once we
see this we can also see that there is no reason to
assume that answering general questions about works
of art in general is somehow necessarily prior to
answering particular questions about particular works
of art. Ohmann is therefore as mistaken in thinking
that we need "a full and convincing explication of
the notion of style" in order to formulate a precise
description of this or that style as Richards was in
thinking that answering "preliminary questions" like
"What *is* a picture, a poem, a piece of music? How
can experiences be compared? What is value?" is
"required in order to approach" questions like "What
gives the experience of reading a certain poem its
value?" *(Principles, pp. 5–6).* Ohmann is of course
quite right in asserting that the metaphorical descriptive terms that interest him "name without explaining," but why is this a defect? If we know the meaning
that a given term ordinarily has in English, what sense
does it make to speak as though the term ought somehow to contain within it a further explanation of
itself or of its application? In practice, of course, we
make clear why we think such terms are applicable
in a given case as Richards did, for example, with the
phrase "sky-scraper hoist": by calling attention (in
Leavis' words) "to this, that or the other detail" of
the poem.[38]

[37] *The Blue and Brown Books* (Oxford: Blackwell, 1958), p. 17.
[38] Stuart Hampshire, in his essay "Logic and Appreciation"
(most readily accessible in William Elton [ed.], *Aesthetics and*

Of course we can make true general statements about works of art: the point is that doing so does not carry us towards the precision the critic seeks. Leavis, replying to Wellek, at one point asked rhetorically:

Has any reader of my book been less aware of the essential criteria that emerge than he would have been if I had laid down such general propositions as: "poetry must be in serious relation to actuality, it must have a firm grasp of the actual, of the object, it must be in relation to life, it must not be cut off from direct vulgar living, it should be normally human . . ."? . . . My whole effort was to work in terms of concrete judgements and particular analyses . . . I feel that by my own methods I have attained a relative precision that makes this summarizing seem intolerably clumsy and inadequate. *[Importance of Scrutiny, pp. 33–34]*

As will by now be clear, I think not only that Leavis is right but also that the difference between generality and critical precision which he is insisting on is precisely the one implied and theoretically explained by the distinction between scientific and critical explanations which emerges from a consideration of Sibley's essay. And yet Leavis' reference to "essential criteria" and his insistence that a certain "consistency . . . and coherence of response," "an organization of similarly 'placed' things" if not "a theoretical system," underlie the critic's judgments makes it clear that he thinks those judgments ought not to be randomly or arbitrarily related to one another. But if this is so— and it certainly seems reasonable enough—the reader might well ask at this point whether there should not

_____

Language [Oxford: Blackwell, 1959], pp. 161–169), makes the theoretical point that seems to be implied in Ohmann's stress on the metaphorical nature of the terms that interest him: a vocabulary made up of such metaphorical terms is somehow unnatural, Hampshire asserts, because it must be formed by the critic acting "in opposition to the main tendency of his language" (pp. 167–168); Sibley answers this charge (effectively, it seems to me) in "Aesthetic Concepts," pp. 441–442.

be some sense in which we can legitimately speak of the critic as proceeding according to principles, some sense in which the word "principle" can legitimately be used about literary criticism. I think the answer is yes, and I should like to conclude by suggesting briefly what sense of the word seems to me appropriate and why.

IV

The sense I have in mind is the one in which R. M. Hare speaks of moral principles in his two books *The Language of Morals* and *Freedom and Reason*. In fact the very first sentence of the former book says in a very general way about morals something like what Leavis is saying about criticism: "If," Hare writes, "we were to ask of a person 'What are his moral principles?' the way in which we could be most sure of a true answer would be by studying what he *did*" *(p. 1)*. Behind Hare's whole view of moral development and moral knowledge rests a plea to speak of moral principles in this way: as what are revealed by what a person actually does in particular situations rather than what he may say—rather, that is, than any set of general propositions or maxims to which he may say he subscribes.

The implication of this way of thinking of principles for Hare's view of moral development is that

> . . . our principles of conduct, as indeed most principles of skill also, are not loose at all. The fact that exceptions are made to them is a sign, not of any essential looseness, but of our desire to make them as rigorous as we can. For what we are doing in allowing classes of exceptions is to make the principle, not looser, but more rigorous. *[Language of Morals, p. 52]*

Hare then gives this example:

> Suppose that we start off with a principle never to say what is false, but regard this principle as provisional, and recognize

that there may be exceptions. Suppose, then, that we decide to make an exception in the case of lies told in war-time to deceive the enemy. The rule has now become "Never say what is false, except in war-time to deceive the enemy." This principle, once the exception has been made explicit and included in the wording of the principle, is not looser than it was before, but tighter. . . .

Thus, far from principles like "Never say what is false" being in some way by nature irredeemably loose, it is part of our moral development to turn them from provisional principles into precise principles with their exceptions definitely laid down; this process is, of course, never completed, but it is always going on in any individual lifetime. If we accept and continue to accept such a principle we cannot . . . break it and leave the principle intact; we have to decide whether to observe the principle and refuse to modify it, or to break it and modify it by admitting a class of exceptions; whereas if the principle were really by nature loose, we could break it without modifying it at all. *[Language of Morals, pp. 52–54]*

The implication of this way of thinking of principles for Hare's view of moral knowledge is that possessing such knowledge is not like having a list of readily statable general propositions constantly and consciously in mind but is, rather, like possessing a complex skill such as driving:

. . . to learn to do anything is never to learn to do an individual act; it is always to learn to do acts of a certain kind in a certain kind of situation; and this is to learn a principle. Thus, in learning to drive, I learn, not to change gear *now*, but to change gear when my engine makes a certain kind of noise. If this were not so, instruction would be of no use at all; for if all an instructor could do were to tell us to change gear *now*, he would have to sit beside us for the rest of our lives in order to tell us just when, on each occasion, to change gear. . . .

The principles that are taught us initially are of a provisional kind (very like the principle "Never say what is false" which I discussed in the last chapter). Our training, after the initial stages, consists in taking these principles, and making them less provisional; we do this by using them continually in our own decisions, and sometimes making exceptions to them . . .

Drivers often know just what to do in a certain situation without being able to enunciate in words the principle on which they act. This is a very common state of affairs with all kinds of principles. . . . One may know how, without being able to say how—though if a skill is to be taught, it is easier if we *can* say how. [*Language of Morals, pp. 60–61, 62, 64*]

Therefore, as he puts it in *Freedom and Reason*, "a moral principle has not got to be highly general or simple, or even formulable in words."[39]

I think the situation in criticism is very similar. The principles we normally start out with are crude maxims—"Metaphysical poetry is better than Romantic poetry," "Only French pianists should play Debussy," "Abstract expressionist painting expresses our age's sense of alienation"—and in the course of our critical development they come to seem (in Leavis' phrase) "intolerably clumsy and inadequate," and so we either qualify them or reject them altogether. Very soon the qualifications become too complex to be formulated in words, and so the principles themselves become (in Richards' phrase) "too intricate to be applied." They pass from being maxims or rules that we apply to works of art from the outside to being internalized dispositions or tendencies to see things a certain way and to choose or evaluate accordingly; they gradually combine and interact to form the special "feel" for the critic's subject-matter which Leavis calls "the immediate sense of value that 'places' the poem." It must be said at once that there is nothing mysterious about this process: it seems mysterious only so long as we adopt a model of criticism that assimilates critical precision to generality, critical insight to knowledge of statable general principles, and critical development to the more or less explicit learning of such principles.[40] As soon as we adopt a more appro-

---

[39] (Oxford: Oxford University Press, 1963), pp. 46–47.

priate model, one that brings out the similarities between critical development and learning a complex skill like driving or cabinet-making or playing the violin, it no longer seems mysterious at all. And the adoption of such a model need not mislead us so long as we bear in mind its limitations: the critic is (for example) quite unlike the cabinet-maker in that although he does not proceed according to simple and general maxims or rules that he can be expected to state, he nonetheless is expected to give reasons for doing what he does and saying what he says, and in fact giving such reasons is part of the critic's job whereas we should expect it of the cabinet-maker only if he were training an apprentice, which is not, strictly speaking, part of his job.

Of course the generalizations that aestheticians like Wellek are looking for are not as crude as "Only French pianists should play Debussy" (which, as anyone who ever heard the late Walter Gieseking play Debussy knows, is plainly false) or "Metaphysical poetry is better than Romantic poetry" (which might at least be debatable but is obviously the sort of broad statistical statement that is of no help in judging particular cases). To say that poetry "must be in relation to life" or "must have a firm grasp of the actual" seems a great deal more sophisticated and promising. Yet it isn't really a great deal more precise or helpful, because whether or not such generalizations will apply in any given case will always be an open question before the fact. It is important to see that the problem is not, as it is so often said to be, a matter of what one's *definition* of terms like "life" or "the actual" is: for even to assume that each of us has, when he uses such terms, a statable and clarifying

[40] For a good treatment of the general error about intelligent behavior which lies behind this sort of assimilation, see Chapter II of Gilbert Ryle's *The Concept of Mind* (London: Hutchinson, 1949).

definition of them in mind is to make a mistake similar to the one we saw Richards, the linguists, and Wellek making about critical principles. Such terms are, by their very nature, open and ambiguous, and their openness and ambiguity are not defects but are rather the source of their usefulness.[41] Therefore while generalizations containing them can be extracted from a critic's practice, as Wellek extracted them from Leavis' book, and while such generalizations can even be true, they will always be curiously vague and unilluminating. As Leavis suggests, they only take on precision of meaning through the way the critic operates in particular cases, and once we know that, we really have little or no use for the generalizations.

Now of course it would be perfectly possible to defend seriously the assumption that the linguists and Richards take as their point of departure, that all existing literary criticism is subjective and impressionistic. Indeed if someone did so, it would probably be as impossible to argue with him as it is to argue with the traditional philosophical skeptic who denies that physical objects exist or that one has any way of being certain there are other minds than one's own. But the curious (and, I think, revealing) fact is that this assumption is almost never seriously defended, that it is accepted unquestioningly and functions merely as a point of departure. Usually it seems to be made not out of a genuine and general dissatisfaction with existing criticism but almost ritualistically. Even Ohmann, in "Generative Grammars and the Concept of Literary Style," just asserts that matters of syntactical complexity "have been hard to approach through conventional methods of analysis" *(p. 430)*, without giving any examples of attempts that have failed. And I have noticed something similar in conversations with

[41] In his well-known essay "Verifiability," Friedrich Waismann discusses what he calls "open-textured" concepts. This essay is most readily accessible in Antony Flew (ed.), *Logic and Language (First Series)* (Oxford: Blackwell, 1955), pp. 117–144.

literary people who feel that somehow linguistics will or ought to be able to help the critic base his intuitions more firmly or explain things he is now unable to explain: asked for an example of a particular critical crux where they think linguistics would offer such help, they invariably produce a case in which they themselves, to their own surprise, turn out to be able to say everything they want to say, and thus their dissatisfaction turns out to be imagined.

The fact of the matter is that criticism, whether of literature or of the other arts, is an autonomous activity and that it has, in the words of W. E. Kennick, "in no way been hampered by the absence of generally applicable canons and norms."[42] It is true of criticism, as it probably is of any other sort of writing, that there is more of it that is bad than is good. I think it is also true that recent philosophers like Sibley and Kennick who have interested themselves in aesthetics can shed a good deal of light on the nature of critical discourse. But I think the value of their work, as opposed to that of most of their predecessors, rests partly on their recognition of the autonomy of criticism and of the consequent futility of any attempt, whether based on an already existing science like linguistics or not, to found some new discipline, whether we call it aesthetics or poetics or stylistics or something else, that will make criticism intellectually respectable in a sense that it isn't now. What we really need is just more good criticism, for, as T. S. Eliot once remarked, in criticism the only method is to be very intelligent.

The desire for such a new discipline and the conviction that its existence is necessary to prevent criticism from being merely (and necessarily) subjective cannot be inspired by a sense that we never agree with each other about works of art or argue fruitfully

[42] "Does Traditional Aesthetics Rest on a Mistake?," *Mind*, LXVII (1958), 331.

about them, because of course we often do both. They seem rather to be inspired by uneasiness at the fact that none of us ever agrees *completely* with anyone else about a work of art (at least if we talk long enough) in the sense that all of us with normal senses and intelligence agree in our perception of the physical world, uneasiness that what Leavis calls the "organization of similarly 'placed' things" is never quite the same for any two people. But is this something to be uneasy about? On the contrary, it seems to me simply an inevitable consequence or manifestation of the fact that all of us develop differently and have different minds and sensibilities.

At the end of my opening chapter I promised to return later to general semantics; in doing so now I am not interested in Korzybski's theoretical mistakes about the nature of language but rather in the disastrous results his theories produce when turned to the moral and social ends he meant them to serve. These results, as we saw most clearly in the case of Hayakawa, mainly follow from the implications of the map analogy, particularly the implication that the main goal of thinking and speaking is simply to provide an accurate description of the world as it changes from moment to moment. Hayakawa does qualify this implication by saying that "maps can be made, even though the territories they stand for are not yet actualities,"[1] but I think this stretches the notion of a map so far as to deprive Korzybski's analogy of the meaning he intended it to have: after all, if the territory does not yet exist, what we draw is not a map but a plan or blueprint. And in fact Hayakawa actually makes this distinction at one point: "Language is not only descriptive, in the sense of supplying verbal 'maps' of nonverbal 'territories,'" he tells us. "It is also prescriptive or directive in the sense of supplying us with verbal 'blueprints' of nonverbal 'territories' which we intend, through our own efforts, to bring into being."[2] But the bad effects of the map analogy can be seen in the fact that when Hayakawa comes to talk about prescriptive language in detail, his main point is that

If it is to influence our conduct, it *must* make use of every affective element in language: dramatic variations in tone of

[1] *Language in Thought and Action,* rev. ed. (New York: Harcourt Brace Jovanovich, 1964), p. 102. As in Chapter I, further quotes will be identified by the initials of the Hayakawa and Chase books.

[2] *Symbol, Status, and Personality* (New York: Harcourt Brace Jovanovich, 1963), p. 108.

voice, rhyme and rhythm, purring and snarling, words with strong affective connotations, endless repetition. If meaningless noises will move the audience, meaningless noises must be made; if facts move them, facts must be given; if noble ideals move them, we must make our proposals appear noble; if they will respond only to fear, we must scare them stiff. *[LTA, p. 102]*

For him "The important question to be asked of any directive utterance is, 'Will things happen as promised if I do as I am directed to do?'" *(LTA, p. 105)*; there is no suggestion that quite aside from a particular goal's chances of achievement, it is often important to ask (and difficult to decide) whether or not it is admirable, and whether the arguments advanced in its favor are sound.

Therefore, though Hayakawa endeavors to reassure us that the self-actualizing or genuinely sane person will not operate in "complete conformity with the goals . . . of [his] society" *(SSP, p. 55)*, he does not go on to say that there are better and worse reasons for being critical of this or that turn of events, but instead quotes A. H. Maslow to the effect that "The fully-functioning personality can be, when the objective situation calls for it, comfortably disorderly, anarchic, vague, doubtful, uncertain, indefinite, approximate, inexact, or inaccurate" *(quoted SSP, p. 61)*. Since being any of these things is quite different from being *intelligently* critical, such lapses from conformity seem more like arbitrary holidays, taken at the bidding of some unspecified "objective situation," than like purposeful actions that we perform as the result of rational decisions we have arrived at for ourselves. And so the troubling question remains: Will this person ever be intelligently critical (or for that matter intelligently withhold criticism) of society, and if so, how will he learn what he needs to know in order to decide when and why and what and whether to criticize?

As we have seen, the consciousness of abstracting

sought by general semanticists is not, in itself, sufficient to produce the tolerance and openmindedness they also seek. For the two complementary aspects of consciousness of abstracting—to borrow de Saussure's terms we might call them its synchronic and diachronic aspects—are an awareness of every object's uniqueness at a given moment and a continuing awareness of universal change, and we have seen that neither the fact that an object is unique nor the fact that a change is occurring has any ethical significance whatever. It is one thing to *perceive* the way in which a particular person or act or situation is different from or similar to others, and quite another to *decide* what course of action these similarities and differences justify and why. This is why it is always logically possible for two people to be in perfect agreement about the facts of a situation and yet, without either of them contradicting himself, to reach different decisions about what ought to be done.

Therefore we must disagree with Hayakawa's confident statement that "morality and ethics come naturally, as the result of proper evaluation"—i.e., of consciousness of abstracting—and that "ordinary 'moral' problems fade out of existence for sane people" *(SSP, p. 68)* because they are "problems we create for ourselves through lack of self-insight" *(SSP, p. 69)*. Surely life isn't this easy. Granted that the "problems" Hayakawa quotes Maslow as citing— "whether or not one plays cards or dances, or wears short or long dresses, exposing the head in some churches and covering it in others, drinking wine, eating some meats and not others, or eating them on some days and not others" *(quoted SSP, p. 68)*—do not present much difficulty for most people, there are a great many other problems, usually called moral and quite real rather than self-created, that do. And it seems obvious that solving them intelligently requires more than sustained appreciative contact with the flux of events. It is all very well for Hayakawa to tell us blandly that "since the map is not the territory, and since, therefore, knowledge about an event is never the event itself, those who take this fact for granted are not uncomfortable about the fact that they don't know the answers" *(SSP, p. 61)*; but sometimes, when confronted by the important public and private questions that come up quite often for all of us, we *should* be uncomfortable about not knowing the answer, and should feel compelled to bring the full weight of our experience and our intelligence to bear in deciding which answer is best and why.

Now as I suggested while discussing Sibley in the preceding chapter, there are important differences between moral and critical language, and some of the failings of earlier attempts at a theory of criticism have been partially due to a failure to take account of these differences. But as I also suggested in discussing what I take to be the appropriate way of talking about principles in criticism, I think there are also important similarities between the two kinds of language and between the two activities we use them to talk about. One of the most important of these similarities is that critical language is, like moral language, prescriptive. Though the nature of perception and the relation of perception to decision or choice are obviously not the same in criticism as in morals, it is nonetheless true that a critical account of a work of art naturally and normally ends in the sort of judgment that Sibley calls a verdict, and that the point of such judgments is (in Hayakawa's phrase) "to influence our conduct." Of course the critic is not usually trying to influence— or at least not directly—our conduct as moral agents but rather to influence the way we shape our imaginative lives; but the line between imaginative life and ordinary or active or "real" life is not always as clear as it might seem to be. Certainly to separate the two realms of ethics and aesthetics completely, as some recent philosophers have attempted to do, is to over-react to the bad old tendency to assimilate the latter to the former.[3] Even the sort of aesthetic judgments (as opposed to verdicts) that interest Sibley are prescriptive in the sense that they are making a claim about what qualities a trained and discriminating observer or reader or listener *ought* to find in the work in question, and any attempt to reduce such judgments to statements that make no such claim—statements, for example, about phonemes or psychological states—will inevitably distort and dilute their meaning by depriving them of a very important part of their content.

Hayakawa, however, wants to go still further than Richards and the linguists and to treat prescriptive language as virtually without content, as an indiscriminate grab-bag of stage-effects ranging from "dramatic variations in tone of voice" all the way down to "meaningless noises"—to be sure "facts" are sometimes to be thrown in, but only for their emotional effect, only if they will "move" the audience. I think our examination of Bloomfieldian linguistics, and of the general conception of science on which it rested, puts us in a position to see this view of prescriptive language in its proper intellectual context, as a grotesque extension of the positivist antipathy to prescription. With the Bloomfieldians, as we saw, this antipathy, which arose out of a perfectly justifiable conviction that science ought to be objective, led to what Chomsky has claimed is an inhibiting notion of the goals and methods of linguistics; with Hayakawa, it leads to the artificial neutrality with which he treated the civil rights issue and finally to utter passivity.

In fact, since moral language is unavoidably prescriptive, the main impression that one gets from

---

[3] For an example of this recent tendency, see Stuart Hampshire, "Logic and Appreciation," in William Elton (ed.), *Aesthetics and Language* (Oxford: Blackwell, 1959), pp. 161–169; for a qualification of Hampshire's view, see W. E. Kennick, "Does Traditional Aesthetics Rest on a Mistake?," *Mind,* LXVII (1958), 327 ff.

Hayakawa's view of prescriptive language, and indeed from his whole attempt to apply Korzybski's theories, is that settling moral questions is not even a rational activity. Of course to believe that it is a rational activity also involves believing that sometimes some answers and arguments will be better than others, and this Hayakawa is usually reluctant to acknowledge— apparently because he fears that doing so would necessarily be dogmatic or intolerant. Instead, as in the case of the white Southerners and the Negro spokesmen, he preserves a strict (and, as we saw, a rather artificial) neutrality. But his fears are unfounded. To be intolerant is to deny other people the right to answer questions for themselves and to attempt to impose our answers on them, while to be dogmatic is to refuse to test our own answers against arguments that lead to different answers. But the fact that we are all free to answer moral questions for ourselves in no way implies that all answers are equally good, and therefore we do not have to remain neutral in order to avoid intolerance. Nor does our sense that it is very important to find the best answers and to be able to justify them imply that we are committed to silencing or persecuting people who disagree with us in order to preserve our answers against their arguments; in fact it implies precisely the opposite: that we are committed to disagreeing with them, either tacitly or openly, unless we find reason to change our minds. Therefore we do not have to remain neutral in order to avoid dogmatism.[4] Whether we are concerned with morals or with criticism, the desirable alternative to intolerance and dogmatism is not neutrality but rather fairness or disinterestedness, which are quite different. Since disagreements, when they come out into the open as

[4] Here I am again indebted to the account of moral reasoning given by R. M. Hare in his two books: *The Language of Morals* (Oxford: Oxford University Press, 1952) and *Freedom and Reason* (Oxford: Oxford University Press, 1963).

clarifying arguments, are necessary to the achievement of fairness or disinterestedness, they are hardly the symptoms of cultural or personal sickness that general semantics takes them to be; far from needing to be eliminated by the "theory of universal agreement" that Korzybski envisioned, they need to be encouraged, for they are one of the main sources of a culture's life.

It may seem surprising that Korzybski's theories, when put into practice, banish morals from the domain of reason, for certainly his aim was precisely to give morals a firm footing by making it scientific. Yet in a curious way science itself is irrational for the general semanticist—it too "comes naturally" as the inevitable result of "proper evaluation." "Kittens and good scientists," Stuart Chase tells us, "tend to let new experience pour in until some kind of workable relationships with past experience are established."[5] But as the passage I quoted from Max Black on pp. 37–38 suggests, the wide-eyed childlike openness recommended by general semanticists as "scientific" and therefore as conducive to sanity is in fact quite inadequate to account for theory construction in science. Once we recognize that the moral growth which we expect of adults, and which general semanticists require for the accomplishment of their social aims, does not "come naturally" as the result of lapsing into silent recognition that Jew_1 is not Jew_2 and that neither of them is today what he was yesterday, we can see that this childlike openness is just as inadequate in morals as in science. The attainment of qualities like tolerance and openmindedness requires cultivating a sense of informed disinterestedness, not merely returning to (or preserving) a state of mindless neutrality or passivity. In turn, that cultivation requires not merely data absorbed passively and word-

[5] *The Tyranny of Words* (New York: Harcourt Brace Jovanovich, 1938), p. 48.

lessly from the outside world but standards, principles, and insights that can only be arrived at by concentrated, active critical thought and argument. In morals (and in criticism) as in science, the important and interesting relationships are not mysteriously "established" for us; it is we who establish them, and we do so by the kind of thinking that both the theory and practice of general semantics tend to discourage.

Therefore the faith that Korzybski and his followers place in science does not imply a faith in what we ordinarily mean by reason, but rather the opposite. Hayakawa writes:

Citizens of a modern society need . . . more than that ordinary "common sense" which was defined by Stuart Chase as that which tells you that the world is flat. They need to be systematically aware of the powers and limitations of symbols, especially words, if they are to guard against being driven into complete bewilderment by the complexity of their semantic environment. [LTA, pp. 29–30]

And Chase himself reminds us that "in the semantic approach to abstractions there is no plea to 'think things through'—the stock retort of one dogmatist to another. 'Thinking things through' has heretofore largely meant more useless mental labor—from thought to word and back to thought again" (TW, pp. 90–91). At one point in Saul Bellow's brilliant short novel Seize the Day a mystical and faintly ominous charlatan named Dr. Tamkin sternly (and with a characteristic air of self-congratulation) addresses Tommy Wilhelm, the book's rather dim but very sympathetic and much abused protagonist: " 'I read the best of literature, science and philosophy,' Dr. Tamkin said. . . . 'Korzybski, Aristotle, Freud, W. H. Sheldon, and all the great poets. You answer me like a layman. You haven't applied your mind strictly to this.' "[6] The allusion to Korzybski has always seemed

[6] (New York: Viking Press, 1956), p. 72.

to me wonderfully apt, for the faith that general semanticists place in science is in fact the result of an extremely pessimistic view of what ordinary thinking, as practiced by "laymen," can ever accomplish.

Moreover, this pessimism is either the cause or the effect, or perhaps both, of Korzybski's whole view of language. Language, we recall, is an abstraction from the ordinary world just as the ordinary world is an abstraction from the scientific world. Since for Korzybski abstraction is merely a matter of omitting characteristics, to speak of language as an abstraction—and even worse, as an abstraction from an abstraction— is to stress its thinness and artificiality, its inability even to reflect faithfully the world as we perceive it, which of course is itself only a pale and dull reflection of the inexhaustibly rich and vivid world known to modern physics. Hence it is not surprising that general semanticists talk a great deal about the limitations of language but very little, and very unconvincingly, about its resources. And since thought only takes shape or actualizes itself in language, to be unaware of the resources of language is to be unaware of the resources of thought.

Though Korzybski's ignorance of history led him to treat this sense of the inadequacy of language as something that he, or at least the twentieth century, had invented, it seems to be as old as systematic thought—probably because it is really just another expression of the feeling everyone who has tried to think systematically has, that thinking is very difficult. What Black has called, in another connection, "the ancient metaphysical lament that to describe is *necessarily* to falsify"[7] is behind Korzybski's strange doctrine that to describe or classify an object is literally to identify it—falsely of course—with the word used to describe or classify it. And anyone who has

---

[7] "Linguistic Relativity: The Views of Benjamin Lee Whorf," in *Models and Metaphors* (Ithaca, N.Y.: Cornell University Press, 1962), p. 248.

read *Gulliver's Travels* will have noticed an earlier (and more extreme) version of Korzybski's view that words ought to (but cannot) "cover" or "include all characteristic of" the objects they refer to in the view of those Laputan professors who, "since words are only names for *things*," devised a "new scheme of expressing themselves by *things*."[8] Even Plato was not above having a little fun at the expense of some of his predecessors, who—despite what Korzybski would no doubt have regarded as the unsane, delusional, unconditionally false-to-fact orientation forced upon them by the Greek language—had managed to come remarkably close to one of the pet dogmas of general semantics. "These wise men," Socrates tells us, held "that nothing *is* one thing, in and of itself, but is always *becoming*, relative to someone, and that 'is' should be completely abolished, though by habit and ignorance we have often been forced to use the word —just now for example."[9]

Most of the bits and pieces of theory that Korzybski patched together to make general semantics can in fact be traced back a good deal further than he or his followers probably realized. For that matter, not even the pseudoscientific mumbo jumbo about the "mad dance of 'electrons' " was original.[10] But I would not want to leave the impression that there is nothing new in general semantics, for this is far from true. What is new—and what is perhaps the central paradox of Korzybski's thought—is that while he seems to be saying that language and thought are intimately and inevitably bound up with one another, he really turns out to be saying just the opposite. While he

[8] Book III, Chapter 6.

[9] *Theaetetus*, 157A–B.

[10] The most famous statement of this influential and persuasive view is in Sir Arthur Eddington's *The Nature of the Physical World* (Cambridge: Cambridge University Press, 1928); its definitive refutation is offered by L. Susan Stebbing in *Philosophy and the Physicists* (London: Methuen, 1937).

seems to be offering us a science of meaning that will help us to use language better than we do, he is really promising a way of getting outside language and its difficulties by giving us what Kenneth Burke once perceptively called "glimpses into an almost mystical cult of silence."[11] Rather in the manner of a tent-show evangelist, Korzybski paints a dire picture of thought enslaved by language and men at the mercy of words, then suddenly provides a battery of theories and techniques that will "automatically" insure salvation. Finally the only real influence of language on thought turns out to be the bad influence it had before we saw the light and returned to a state of passive and uncritical contact with "the nonverbal level, where," Chase rhapsodically writes, "one can point but cannot utter, the very threshold where the senses make contact with the outside world" (*TW, p. 39*).

I think we can begin to understand both the immense popularity of general semantics and its importance as a peculiarly American cultural symptom if we look closely at the way Chase describes this wordless state:

> This contact comes before language and cannot be spoken. The eye receives light-waves from the apple, but says nothing. This apple, any apple, any object or act, is on the nonverbal level. Here we see it as a cat sees it, quietly and without words. . . . Here is the base from which all our proud words rise—every last one of them—and to it they must constantly return and be refreshed. [*TW, p. 39*]

Plainly this allegorical journey that general semanticists are always inviting us to take is a return to innocence—in this case, to an Eden complete with apple. But unlike other earlier journeys of return, this one will end in an innocence shared not only by

[11] *A Grammar of Motives* (Englewood Cliffs, N.J.: Prentice-Hall, 1945), p. 239.

"kittens" but by "good scientists" as well. By presenting scientific observation as the highest form of primal innocence, general semanticists make their evangelism sound deceptively modern and tough-minded, reassuring us of the value and accessibility of the simpler life they offer and making it easier to justify our longing for a release from what Sir Joshua Reynolds once called "the real labor of thinking."

Now to discourage people from engaging in "the real labor of thinking," and specifically to discourage them from engaging in the sort of critical thought about morals or about literature and the other arts needed to achieve informed disinterestedness, is a dangerous business. I have tried to suggest that despite their very great differences general semantics, American descriptive linguistics, and the attempt to put literary criticism on some sort of scientific basis are closely interrelated. Despite the exciting and enduring practical achievements of descriptive linguists, the view of science on which their work officially rests, by emphasizing almost exclusively the role of observation in science, opened the way not only for the general semanticists' *reductio ad absurdum* of science to silence but also (and more importantly) for the far more sophisticated (and therefore culturally more dangerous) scientism of Richards and the linguists whose work we reviewed in the preceding chapter. For scientism, as it is usually defined, is the belief that there is one method which is common to all the sciences and which ought to be applied in all other fields of inquiry as well. And since observation does in fact play some part not only in all formal fields of inquiry but also in most ordinary everyday activities, to emphasize it exclusively as what makes science scientific is to encourage scientism. In the past, people professionally concerned with literature who have opposed efforts to make literary criticism scientific have usually (and often with a good deal of justice) been accused of being in one way or another "against science"; in building my own case for opposing such efforts, I hope I have convinced the reader that I am merely against the sort of blurring of boundaries and disregard for fact that is inimical not only to science but also to ordinary common sense.

SELECTED BIBLIOGRAPHY

What follows is intended neither as an exhaustive bibliography nor as a "list of works cited," but rather as a very selective working bibliography for further reading. Thus while most of the books listed have been referred to in the text, some have not. All of the journal articles I wished to list have been reprinted, either in collection or anthology form; since in their reprinted form they are most readily available to the general reader, it is in that form that they are listed. Moreover, I wanted to call to the attention of the reader these anthologies since most of them are excellent, not only because of the other articles they include but also because of their often extensive bibliographies.

Alston, William P. *Philosophy of Language.* Englewood Cliffs, N.J.: Prentice-Hall, 1964.

Austin, J. L. *Philosophical Papers,* J. O. Urmson and G. J. Warnock (eds.). Oxford: Oxford University Press, 1961.

_____. *How to Do Things with Words.* J. O. Urmson (ed.). Cambridge, Mass.: Harvard University Press, 1962.

Barrett, Cyril (ed.). *Collected Papers on Aesthetics.* New York: Barnes & Noble, 1966. Includes Sibley's "Aesthetic Concepts" and W. E. Kennick's "Does Traditional Aesthetics Rest on a Mistake?".

Bentley, Eric (ed.). *The Importance of Scrutiny.* New York: Grove Press, 1957. Includes Leavis' controversy with Wellek.

Black, Max. *Language and Philosophy.* Ithaca, N.Y.: Cornell University Press, 1949.

_____. *Models and Metaphors.* Ithaca, N.Y.: Cornell University Press, 1962.

Bloch, Bernard, and George L. Trager. *Outline of Linguistic Analysis.* Baltimore: Linguistic Society of America, 1942.

Bloomfield, Leonard. *Language.* New York: Holt, Rinehart & Winston, 1933.

Casey, John. *The Language of Criticism.* London: Methuen, 1966.

Caton, Charles E. (ed.). *Philosophy and Ordinary Language.* Urbana: University of Illinois Press, 1963. Includes Austin's "The Meaning of a Word," and Ryle's "Ordinary Language" and "The Theory of Meaning."

Chappell, V. C. (ed.). *Ordinary Language.* Englewood Cliffs, N.J.: Prentice-Hall, 1964. Includes Ryle's "Ordinary Language," Austin's "A Plea For Excuses," and Stanley Cavell's "Must We Mean What We Say?".

Chomsky, Noam. *Syntactic Structures.* The Hague: Mouton, 1957.

_____. *Current Issues in Linguistic Theory*. The Hague: Mouton, 1964.

_____. *Aspects of the Theory of Syntax*. Cambridge, Mass.: M.I.T. Press, 1965.

_____. *Cartesian Linguistics*. New York: Harper & Row, 1966.

_____. *Language and Mind*. New York: Harcourt Brace Jovanovich, 1968.

Fann, K. T. (ed.). *Ludwig Wittgenstein: The Man and His Philosophy*. New York: Dell, 1967.

_____. (ed.). *Symposium on J. L. Austin*. New York: Humanities Press, 1969.

Fodor, Jerry A., and Jerrold J. Katz (eds.). *The Structure of Language*. Englewood Cliffs, N.J.: Prentice-Hall, 1964. Includes the editors' "The Structure of a Semantic Theory," and Chomsky's *Current Issues in Linguistic Theory*, "A Transformational Approach to Syntax," and review of B. F. Skinner's *Verbal Behavior*.

Hare, R. M. *The Language of Morals*. Oxford: Oxford University Press, 1952.

Harris, Zellig S. *Methods in Structural Linguistics*. Chicago: University of Chicago Press, 1951. Later editions entitled *Structural Linguistics*.

Hungerland, Isabel C. *Poetic Discourse*. University of California Publications in Philosophy, Volume 33. Berkeley, Cal.: University of California Press, 1958.

Joos, Martin (ed.). *Readings in Linguistics*, 2d ed. New York: American Council of Learned Societies, 1958.

Katz, Jerrold J. *The Philosophy of Language*. New York: Harper & Row, 1966.

Leavis, F. R. *Education and the University*. London: Chatto & Windus, 1943. Includes "Literary Studies."

Lyons, John. *Noam Chomsky*. New York: Viking Press, 1970.

Mace, C. A. (ed.). *British Philosophy in the Mid-Century*. London: Allen and Unwin, 1957. Includes Ryle's "The Theory of Meaning" and Stuart Hampshire's "The Interpretation of Language: Words and Concepts."

Malcolm, Norman. *Ludwig Wittgenstein: A Memoir*. Includes a biographical sketch by G. H. von Wright. London: Oxford University Press, 1958.

Mitchell, David. *An Introduction to Logic*. London: Hutchinson, 1962.

Passmore, John. *A Hundred Years of Philosophy*. London: Duckworth, 1957. 2d rev. ed., London: Duckworth, 1966; Harmondsworth, Middlesex: Penguin Bks. 1968.

Pears, David. *Ludwig Wittgenstein*. New York: Viking Press, 1969.

Pitcher, George. *The Philosophy of Wittgenstein*. Englewood Cliffs, N.J.: Prentice-Hall, 1964.

_____. (ed.). *Wittgenstein: The "Philosophical Investigations."* Garden City, N.Y.: Anchor Books, 1966.

Richards, I. A. *Principles of Literary Criticism*, 3d ed. New York: Harcourt Brace Jovanovich, 1928.

_____. *Practical Criticism*. London: Routledge & Kegan Paul, 1929.

Ryle, Gilbert. *The Concept of Mind*. London: Hutchinson, 1949.

Sapir, Edward. *Language*. New York: Harcourt Brace Jovanovich, 1921.

Saussure, Ferdinand de. *Course in General Linguistics*. Wade Baskin, trans. New York: Philosophical Library, 1959.

Sebeok, Thomas A. (ed.). *Style in Language*. New York: Technology Press of M.I.T. and John Wiley, 1960.

Urmson, J. O. *Philosophical Analysis*. Oxford: Oxford University Press, 1956.

Warnock, G. J. *English Philosophy Since 1900*. London: Oxford University Press, 1958.

Wittgenstein, Ludwig. *Philosophical Investigations*. German with English translation by G. E. M. Anscombe. Oxford: Blackwell, 1953. 2d rev. ed. Oxford: Blackwell, 1958.

_____. *The Blue and Brown Books*. Oxford: Blackwell, 1958.

_____. *Zettel*. G. E. M. Anscombe and G. H. von Wright (eds.). German with English translation by G. E. M. Anscombe. Oxford: Blackwell, 1967.

INDEX

Ogden, C. K., 36n., 143, 145
Ohmann, Richard, 118–119, 134–141, 148, 152, 168
Ordinary language philosophy, 34–35, 60–61, 91, 106, 109–115
Osborne, Harold, 159

Pāṇini, 69
Pearson, Karl, 71–72
Picture theory of meaning, 53–54
Pitcher, George, 61n., 107n.
Plato, 186
Pollock, Jackson, 165
Port Royal Grammar, 65
Positivism, 71–73
Postal, Paul M., 85n., 103n.
Putnam, Hilary, 104n.

Reynolds, Sir Joshua, 188
Richards, I. A., xv, xviii, 36n., 118–119, 141–156, 158–159, 163–166,
    168, 172, 174, 181, 188
Riffaterre, Michael, 120
Rosenberg, Harold, 165
Rules (vs. regularities), 73, 90–94
Russell, Bertrand, 21
Ryle, Gilbert, 28n., 34–35n., 60, 110–114, 173n.

Saporta, Sol, 121–122
Saussure, Ferdinand de, 62–65, 78–81, 83, 86–87, 108, 179
    and Bloomfield, 63–65, 78
    and Chomsky, 78–87
    on "general grammar," 68
    on history of linguistics, 63–65
    on *langue* and *parole*, 79–81
    on linguistics as a science, 63, 65, 79–81
Schwyzer, H. G. R., 161n.
Searle, John, 92–94, 107n.
Semantics
    in American descriptive (structural) linguistics, 75–77, 95–97,
        99–100, 118
    in Chomskyan (transformational) linguistics, 94–106, 110–111,
        115, 118, 141
    and criticism, xvi–xviii, 117–177
    general, *see* General semantics
    in Richards' work, *see* Richards, I. A.
Shakespeare, 126, 134
Shelley, 127–128
Sibley, Frank, 161–169, 180–181
Skinner, B. F., 100n.